Enrichment Magazine

IN THIS ISSUE . . .

iStockphoto.com

© Fausto Renda/Shutterstock, Inc.

To the Director

This student folder contains nine study leaflets and the enrichment magazine. Remove the center staple and distribute the leaflets as indicated in the leaders guide. This magazine should be distributed at the first session for use throughout the course.

I0806848

3558 S. Jefferson Ave., St. Louis, MO 63118-3968

1-800-325-3040 • www.cph.org

Written by Mark B. Stirdivant

Edited by Edward A. Engelbrecht

Cover: The Ghent Altarpiece (1425–32), Hubert van Eyck, detail. Iberfoto / Iberfoto

Graphic design by Christina Ensign

This publication may be available in Braille, in large print, or on cassette tape for the visually impaired. Please allow 8 to 12 weeks for delivery. Write to Lutheran Braille Workers, P.O. Box 5000, Yucaipa, CA 92399; call toll-free 1-800-925-6092; or visit the Web site: www.LBWinc.org.
Manufactured in the United States of America

1 2 3 4 5 6 7 8 9 10 24 23 22 21 20 19 18 17 16 15

Juri Pozzi/iStockphoto.com

What's Wrong with EDOM?

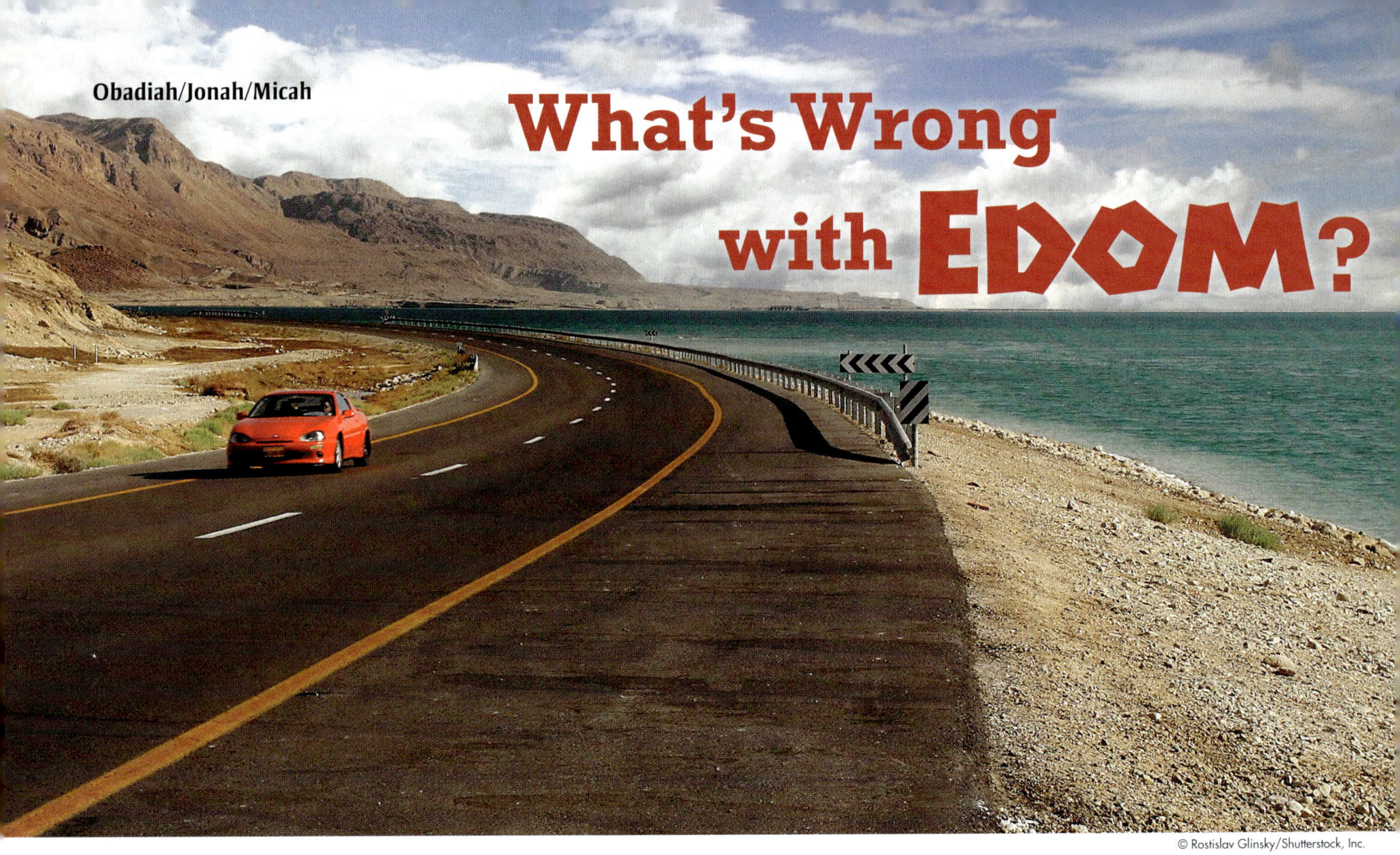

© Rostislav Glinsky/Shutterstock, Inc.

It will take you most of a day to drive here from the population centers of Jordan. You will travel a lonely, four-lane highway that traces the ancient King's Highway, heading due south through a rocky, mountainous wilderness. The next day, you will hike through a narrow split in the sandy cliffs, and suddenly a magnificent edifice will emerge into view. It looks like a two-story Greek temple carved out of the rock. Known as "the Treasury," it is the centerpiece of dazzling red stone remains of the once-thriving city of Petra.

The Nabatean civilization was responsible for these engineering wonders. The Nabateans were known for building grand cities nestled high on cliffs. Before their arrival, this particular land was controlled by a more nomadic collection of tribes—the Edomites. The prophet Obadiah knew all too well how the people of Israel had struggled with the people of Edom for some 1,400 years.

Red and Rugged

Edom means "red," which makes this ruddy landscape a perfect environment for a people descended from the Bible's first known redhead—Esau. Genesis 25 tells us of the tumultuous relationship between the twins Jacob and Esau that started even before they were born. The firstborn came out of the womb red and hairy; he was destined to become a lover of hunting and pushing the limits of survival. Then arrived Jacob, grabbing Esau's heel; he preferred staying close to home, waiting for his chance to gain the advantage that the Lord prophesied he would eventually attain.

Jacob succeeded, thanks to two events involving food. He conned the famished Esau out of his birthright with some red stew (Genesis 25:33). Then, with the assistance of his mother, Jacob dressed in goatskins and Esau's smelly clothes and served a meal to blind Isaac in order to receive the firstborn's blessing (Genesis 27). For a long time, Esau committed himself to vengeance against his deceptive brother, and Jacob fled for his life away from the Promised Land in order to work for his uncle Laban.

Edom vs. Israel

Long after Jacob's vision of a ladder to heaven (Genesis 28), the Lord gave him the grace of reconciliation with his estranged brother Esau (Genesis 33). The brothers agreed to live apart, similar to the decision of Abraham and Lot over a century before, since their abundant possessions and families made it impossible to dwell in the same land together. This time, it was Jacob who inhabited the better land, while Esau took his entourage southward into the hilly, red-rocked wilderness formerly known as Seir, the "shaggy mountain." The Edomites could not survive in this environment through farming or herding sheep, but they fortunately discovered an abundance of copper deposits, which was a valuable commodity during the Bronze Age.

© Gigi Peis/Shutterstock, Inc.

For centuries, both families left each other alone and grew into great nations. Because Israel moved to Egypt at Joseph's invitation, Edom did not have much contact with their ancient cousins, except of course to buy grain from Joseph during the severe famine, which had affected the whole earth (Genesis 41:57). The Lord would not allow them to return into conflict until after the exodus.

A resumed conflict couldn't have come at a worse time. Numbers 20 includes some significant turning points for the wandering Israelites. Moses' sister Miriam died (v. 1), as did his brother Aaron (v. 28). Moses disobeyed the Lord by striking the rock of Meribah instead of speaking to it as God had commanded (vv. 6–13), thereby disqualifying himself from setting foot in the Promised Land. Right in the midst of all this turmoil, Moses sent a delegation of messengers to the king of Edom, since the traveling nation of millions had finally reached Edom's border. Even though Israel had promised to travel straight through, not to disturb a single field, vineyard, or even a well, nevertheless, Edom absolutely forbade any Israelites from taking even one step on their soil. The king of Edom showed up with a massive army in order to enforce the prohibition. This forced the entire Israelite entourage to turn back on their route to Canaan so that they would bypass Edom. Of course, the people complained some more about their worsening circumstances. In response to their complaints, the Lord sent a plague of serpents to humble them—but then He gave a sign to comfort and heal (Numbers 21:5–9; notice how this pointed forward to Jesus in John 3:14–15). Perhaps the bronze serpent was made using Edom's copper? It can only be a guess.

Corbert Gauthier © CPH

The next significant contact between Israel and Edom recorded in Scripture is when King David subdued his neighbors to the south, taking home their silver and gold, erecting garrisons in their territory, and forcing the Edomites to serve him. In fact, his single-battle success in the Valley of Salt claimed 18,000 of their soldiers and established an even stronger reputation for the slayer of Goliath (2 Samuel 8:11–14). Edom had its chance to retaliate against Israel once its exiled leader Hadad returned from Egypt and Israel's crown passed from David to Solomon. However, not much gain could be made for Edom until well into the time of the Divided Kingdom, when the descendants of Esau finally threw off the yoke of David's heavy-handed rule (2 Kings 8:20–22) and gained independence for about a century.

Kick While They're Down

In the 700s BC, two centuries before Obadiah, a new foreign power arrived on the scene—the Assyrians. They had an overwhelming army that was intent on conquering the entire Middle East. In 722, the Northern Kingdom of Israel fell to Assyria and was scattered. To the few Israelites who were allowed to remain, Assyria introduced settlers from other parts of its expanding empire; the resulting half-Jew/half-Gentile people came to be known as Samaritans. Edom, by contrast, seemed to have a better relationship with Assyria at this time. Sure, they were conquered; their independence was taken away again. But the Edomite rulers welcomed the occupation and paid their dues to their overlords so that Edom fared well, considering that it was now a vassal nation.

Then Assyria was bested by an even bigger empire, from even farther away, and with an even bigger army. Nebuchadnezzar and his Babylonian forces rose up against Assyria, so that by the early sixth century BC, the entire land was under Babylonian control. Any people who survived Nebuchadnezzar's initial sweep were carted off into exile in Babylon, never to return to their homeland. When finally the Babylonian army laid siege to the well-protected city of Jerusalem, it seems that Edom saw an opportunity to gain a profitable alliance with the new boss in town.

The historical records found in 2 Kings 25 and 2 Chronicles 36 speak of only the Babylonians (also called Chaldeans) mercilessly destroying Jerusalem, burning it down into a smoldering rubble. Horrific murder, rape, and even baby-killing fulfilled all the destruction that God had predicted for Jerusalem and its inhabitants, as spoken through centuries of prophets. Yet we find out that the Babylonians were not alone. Prominent among the other surrounding nations who joined the feeding frenzy against the Southern Kingdom of Judah was none other than Edom. They "acted revengefully against the house of Judah and . . . grievously offended in taking vengeance on them" (Ezekiel 25:12).

The Edomite forces were likely just as bloodthirsty as the Babylonians, as Ezekiel stated in his indictment:

Blood shall pursue you; because you did not hate bloodshed. . . . Because you said, "These two nations [likely referring to Israel and Judah separately] . . . shall be mine, and we will take possession of them"—although the Lord *was there—therefore, as I live, declares the Lord* God, *I will deal with you according to the anger and envy that you showed because of your hatred against them. (Ezekiel 35:6, 10–11)*

The notorious imprecatory Psalm 137 makes our ears tingle with revulsion to this very day when it cries out in agony for vengeance against the Edomites who cheered for violence while the Babylonians took the Jewish little ones and dashed them against the rocks.

God Will Have the Final Word!

The tiny Book of Obadiah has a mighty message directed against the vicious and self-confident nation of Edom. Their protective cliff-dwellings, their roaring economy in copper, and their strategic treaties with the highest bidder will not earn them any respite from their impending judgment at the hands of the Lord of all the earth. God's own retribution would pursue the greed and bloodlust of Esau's children in order to prove His claim: "vengeance is Mine."

But the final word does not fall on vengeance. There is a plan for all the world, even those scattered among the evil Edomites, that any who repent and turn by faith to the Messiah, Jesus, even they, will be restored in forgiveness to everlasting life in His spiritual kingdom. When bitter, long-time enemies confront us in our lives and even in our families, our only help is in the Lord who gave His life for our reconciliation with the Father and with one another.

Nineveh

Tigris River

A horrible, bloodthirsty army of invaders established their home base right on the doorstep of Israel. As the eighth century BC dawned, the conquerors were encroaching on their next target: the Northern Kingdom's capital of Samaria. The Assyrians, led by talented military generals and driven by forceful kings, were ready to take over the Middle Eastern world with a success that would have rivaled King David's a couple of centuries before. No one in his right mind would ever wander up to the gates of Assyria's capital, Nineveh, and expect to survive, especially if he were to proclaim a message of doom for hundreds of thousands. Entering those gates of doom would be like . . . getting swallowed by a whale!

Mesopotamian Metropolis

If an ancient world city had a reliable source of water and adequate protection, it would have a fighting chance to survive and even thrive. Nineveh was well-equipped with the advantages of its prime location. Situated on the Tigris River in the foothills of the Kurdish mountains, the area around Nineveh seemed to attract large populations throughout history. Today the Iraqi city of Mosul can be found on the adjacent bank of the river.

The earliest biblical mention of Nineveh is found in Genesis 10, which tells briefly about the city's founder, Nimrod, a descendant of Noah's son Ham. This mighty hunter Nimrod, Moses noted from his records, established a notorious reputation for himself. His early kingdom included cities like Babel (Genesis 10:10–12), but then he moved upriver to found Nineveh and the surrounding cities that later would become its suburbs.

For centuries, Nineveh operated like a city-state, with its own king and military. This was probably what it was like when Jonah preached in Nineveh. Other cities became allies with Nineveh by treaty or intermarriage of its leaders and their family members. When the great Assyrian king Sennacherib took over Nineveh in the early seventh century BC, shortly after Jonah's time, he expanded its size, made significant improvements, and dubbed it his capital city. Since his hilly estates were higher in elevation than the Tigris, he constructed an aqueduct to water his massive gardens, using mountain springs that were several miles away.

Hotbed of Wickedness

It was during this opulent heyday that Nineveh multiplied not only its population but also its evil. According to the writings of the prophets Nahum and Zephaniah, both of whom appeared more than a century and a half after Jonah, the Ninevite repentance that the earlier, reluctant prophet witnessed was at best short-lived. God had seen wickedness in the city sufficient enough to send Jonah to warn of destruction, but He later inspired Nahum to condemn the violence and sexual perversion of the "bloody city" (Nahum 3).

Nineveh and the rest of the Assyrian war machine had many victories upon which they could consider themselves secure. They boasted of the superiority of Ishtar and other Assyrian gods over the deities whom they supposed had tried to defend their opponents. Worship at the temple of Ishtar included prostitution and other immorality. The riches of their own land and the plunder of their conquests only increased their stench in the nostrils of the one true God. In 612 BC, the destruction that was temporarily

Temple of Ishtar ruins

averted in the days of Jonah became the final chapter for a once-great ancient city. At one time they had boasted, "I am, and there is no one else," but suddenly their cedar-clad palaces became a haunt for owls and pastureland for wandering herds (Zephaniah 2:13–15). A lair for wild beasts took the place of lavish halls that echoed with the cheers of exultation and debauchery.

The Word to All Nations

It may not make much sense to us that despite all that Jonah had to endure, his preaching ended up buying only a little time for Nineveh before the inevitable happened. If he had lived long enough, the prophet could have been tempted to say, "See, God? I told You that those people wouldn't listen!"

But what about today? Who do you think is beyond the possibility of repentance unto the forgiveness of sins and everlasting salvation? What causes us to judge people in this way?

Jesus Christ used the example of the people of Nineveh when He rebuked His self-righteous, unbelieving critics. Matthew 12:41 records our Lord's words: "The men of Nineveh will rise up at the judgment with this generation and condemn it, for they repented at the preaching of Jonah, and behold, something greater than Jonah is here." Even though Nineveh and the rest of Assyria did not remain faithful to Almighty God in their succeeding generations, the Lord nevertheless extended His love toward His children, whom He alone knows and whom He alone has called to faith by His sheer grace.

God's judgment and time reduced great and mighty Nineveh to a mere two mounds with a mosque that was originally a Christian church. Recently, even those remains were further destroyed by murderous insurgents. Yet, in God's wisdom alone, when His mouthpiece Jonah preached in its streets, the time was right for His Word to take root and produce faith in His mercy. Despite all the wickedness of the city and its corresponding nation, God desired to show great pity toward those who could not tell their right hand from their left, and even their animals (Jonah 4:11). Jesus earned life-giving forgiveness on the cross for people of all nations—that message is true just as much for us as it was long ago with Jonah. No one, not even a Ninevite, is out of the reach of the Gospel!

Repentance: Ours and God's

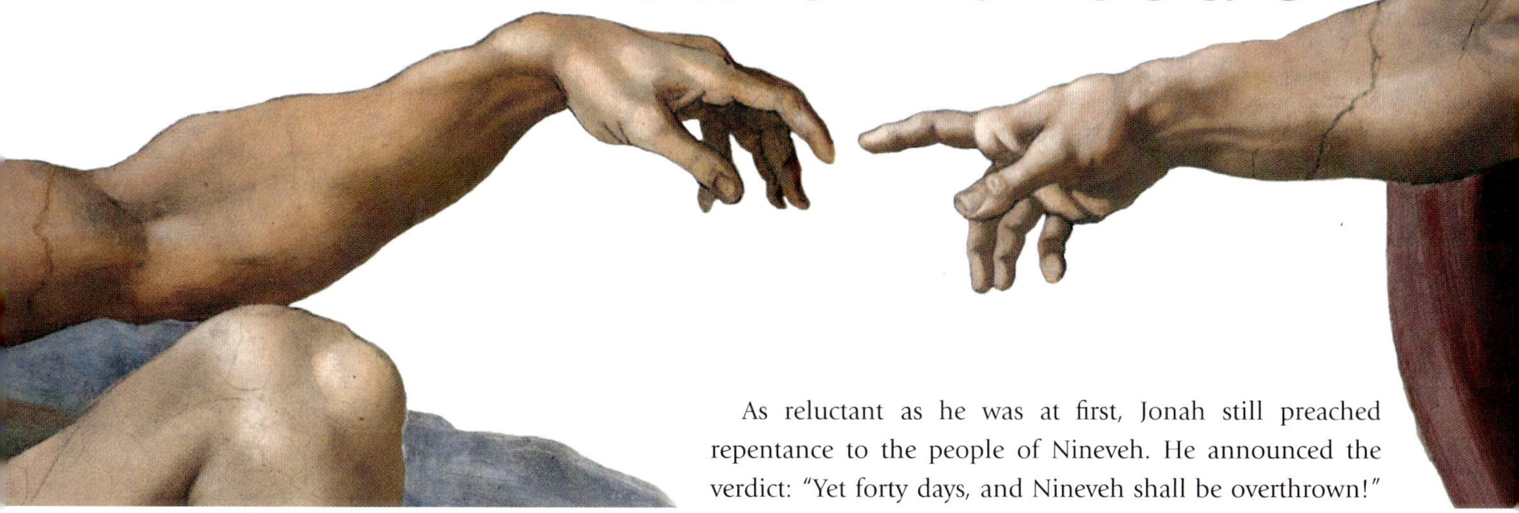

As reluctant as he was at first, Jonah still preached repentance to the people of Nineveh. He announced the verdict: "Yet forty days, and Nineveh shall be overthrown!" (Jonah 3:4). Upon hearing that real threat of divine punishment, the people and their king turned from their sinful ways, which is what it means for people to repent. For example, Obadiah prescribed repentance to the Edomites in the form of certain actions that God required of them: "Do not gloat . . . do not rejoice over the people of Judah in the day of their ruin . . . do not boast . . . do not gloat . . . do not loot" (Obadiah 12–13). Micah said that God preferred genuine fruits of repentance even over "thousands of rams, with ten thousands of rivers of oil" (see Micah 6:6–8). Repentance is necessary for us human beings so that by faith alone we would take hold of Christ and receive deliverance from our deserved punishment. That deliverance, strange as it may sound, involves a form of repentance on God's part.

Pleading for Mercy

One of the best biblical case studies in repentance is King David (see 2 Samuel 11–12 and Psalm 51). David is remembered as a righteous man whom God proclaimed to be "a man after His own heart" (1 Samuel 13:14). Yet David sinned grievously against the Lord when he committed adultery with Bathsheba and then arranged for the murder of her husband, Uriah, a faithful and devoted soldier for Israel. God moved the prophet Nathan to call David to repentance, much as a pastor would today. Through Nathan's touching story about a lamb, the king's righteous anger was incited—against himself! The drama reached its peak when Nathan pierced through David's deception and plainly accused him of adultery and murder: "You are the man!" (2 Samuel 12:7; cf. Matthew 18:15).

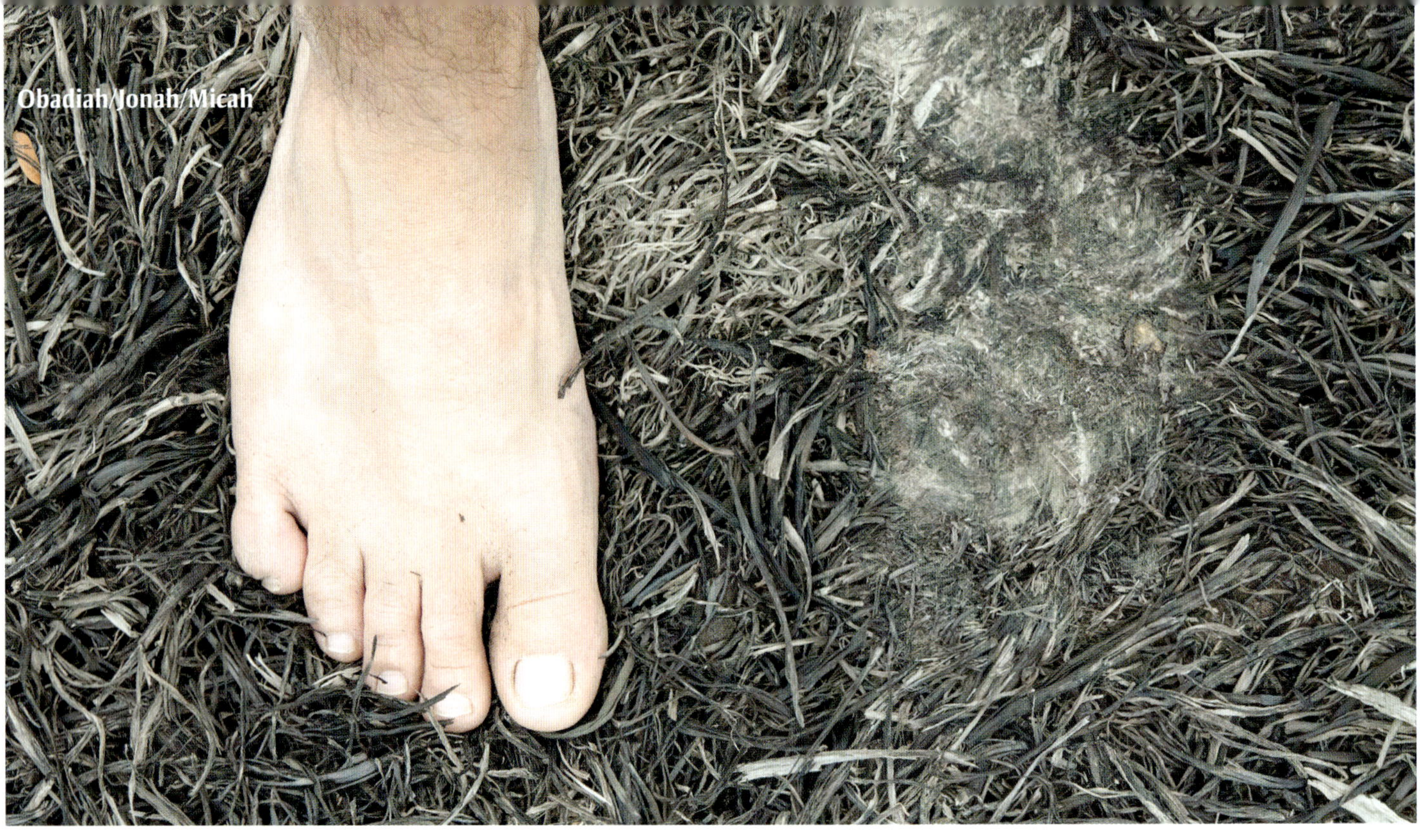

Once Bathsheba bore David's son, who immediately became sick, David grieved over his iniquity and went without food or fun. No doubt he was praying fervently for forgiveness, probably using phrases that he would soon record in what would become Psalm 51. He pleaded for the little child's life, urging the Lord out of mercy to spare the innocent. When the boy died, however, David surprisingly gave up his outward signs of repentance and praised the Lord instead. His puzzled servants asked him why he acted this way, and the king admitted that while the child was still alive, he had this thought: "Who knows whether the LORD will be gracious to me, that the child may live?" (2 Samuel 12:22) But when the child was dead, David reasoned: "I shall go to him, but he will not return to me" (v. 23).

Punishments Averted

What led David to expect that God would change His mind? The death sentence had already been pronounced; the son produced by the adultery was to die. And yet, take note that the repentant king held out some kind of hope, even if he had prefaced it with the same words that the king of Nineveh would say after hearing Jonah's prophecy: "Who knows" (Jonah 3:9). David knew it was better to fall into the hand of God rather than the hand of man. He was fully aware that mercy was the Lord's true nature and that when it came to dishing out punishment, there was at least the possibility He would change His mind—yes, even God is known to repent!—not from sin, but rather from the punishment that He had threatened.

Long before the time of King David, Moses actually dared to ask the Lord to repent (see Psalm 90:13). When the twelve Israelite spies returned from Canaan to make their report, all but two of them spread the news that made the multitude tremble in fear over the armies of giants and their well-protected cities. Most of the people were ready to turn back, replace Moses with a new leader, and return to Egypt after dwelling for a year in the wilderness. God's first reaction to this request was to strike all the people down. However, it was Moses who urged the Lord to reconsider His decision, appealing to God's own reputation among all the Gentile nations:

> *Now if You kill this people as one man, then the nations who have heard Your fame will say, "It is because the LORD was not able to bring this people into the land that He swore to give to them that He has killed them in the wilderness." (Numbers 14:15–16)*

But Moses did not stop there. He pointed out that the greater reason for God to repent—that is, to abandon His threat to punish—is that His love and mercy always have the upper hand over against His justice and retribution. The Lord is known to be "slow to anger and abounding in steadfast love, forgiving iniquity and transgression, but He will by no means clear the guilty" (Numbers 14:18). This one-sentence creed that emphasizes mercy over justice is repeated in the Old Testament, and God demonstrated it many times.

A Greater Plan at Work

God's "repentance" reveals to us that He has more in mind than just to punish the wicked. For example, righteous King Hezekiah was afflicted with a kind of skin disease so severe that God had sent Isaiah the prophet to advise him to set his house in order and prepare for his death (2 Kings 20). Hezekiah prayed a deeply emotional prayer, repenting over the pride in his heart with which the Lord was displeased. Again, the Lord Himself repented from letting Hezekiah die. He allowed Hezekiah to recover and live another fifteen years. God's mercy toward Hezekiah preserved the Southern Kingdom of Judah from the conquering Assyrians and temporarily saved Jerusalem, David's city, because of His promise of the coming Messiah.

During Hezekiah's post-illness "grace period," there was born to him a son, Manasseh. The boy was only twelve years old when his father died and he acceded the throne. Then he actually outdid the evil for which God had long ago punished and removed the other nations that had lived in the Promised Land. The judgment against Manasseh seemed to be the last word: he was captured by the Assyrians and deposited in Babylon, bound with bronze chains (see 2 Chronicles 33).

Whether he knew it or not, Manasseh followed in his father's footsteps of repentance. The Chronicler recorded the drastic turnaround:

> *And when [Manasseh] was in distress, he entreated the favor of the LORD his God and humbled himself greatly before the God of his fathers. He prayed to Him, and God was moved by his entreaty and heard his plea and brought him again to Jerusalem into his kingdom. Then Manasseh knew that the LORD was God. (2 Chronicles 33:12–13)*

The former idolater did "come trembling," and he did "turn in dread to the LORD," as Micah prescribed for the nations (7:17). He instituted a near-thorough reformation of his kingdom's worship, and he commanded all his subjects to sacrifice only to the Lord, the God of Israel and Judah.

Repentance and You

Rituals like sackcloth and ashes (even on beasts; Jonah 3:8!) can be used properly when they reveal a true faith, not just empty ceremonialism. No matter how far sinners have gone astray, God promises to "repent" from punishment whenever they turn to Him, in order for forgiveness to have the final word. This day, indeed every day, make repentance a priority in your life (cf. Matthew 6:11–12). The Lord wants to forgive and restore you as His beloved child. Call on Him with all sincerity.

© iStockphoto.com © Ricardo Reitmeyer/Shutterstock, Inc.

LAW AND GOSPEL EVANGELISM

© Shutterstock, Inc.

God's actions toward us may sometimes seem totally arbitrary. It's like He's constantly changing, or even reversing course. One day, the Lord wipes out nearly 15,000 Israelites in the wilderness, threatening to extinguish all of them (Numbers 16:45), but the very next day, He continues to supply manna so that the survivors could resume their journey well-fed. Jonah doesn't understand why he had to waste time and a three-day fish-belly tour of the Mediterranean just to watch the evil city of Nineveh not get overthrown. And Obadiah's sudden change in tone toward Israel's contentious cousins, the Edomites, reveals that a greater plan than mere retribution is in the works as far as God is concerned.

These drastic differences and apparent contradictions that we encounter in the Bible would remain hidden mysteries for us if God did not uncover His master key to understanding and applying all of Scripture: the distinction between Law and Gospel. Both the Law and the Gospel are His perfect and unassailable Word, and are statements intended for our learning. Yet both also need to be fully understood in their relationship with each other as well as in their particular application to us. Distinguishing Law and Gospel uncovers many interesting things about books that most people ignore, while at the same time the technique opens for pastors and laypeople alike an essential tool to share the saving truths of God in their various contexts. This is the heart of evangelism—that is, proclaiming the good news.

The early Lutheran reformers were fully aware of how important this tool was for the survival of the rightly teaching Church:

> *The distinction between the Law and the Gospel is a particularly brilliant light. It serves the purpose of rightly dividing God's Word [2 Timothy 2:15] and properly explaining and understanding the Scriptures of the holy prophets and apostles. We must guard this distinction with special care, so that these two doctrines may not be mixed with each other, or a law be made out of the Gospel. When that happens, Christ's merit is hidden and troubled consciences are robbed of comfort, which they otherwise have in the Holy Gospel when it is preached genuinely and purely. For by the Gospel they can support themselves in their most difficult trials against the Law's terrors.* (FC SD V 1; Concordia, 552)

Strike the Balance

God's Word often proclaims Law and Gospel in a particular order for a reason. God assures us: "As I live, declares the Lord GOD, I have no pleasure in the death of the wicked, but that the wicked turn from his way and live" (Ezekiel 33:11). World salvation, in which our Lord has graciously involved us, is God's goal. Yet before a sinner can trust in Jesus, who is revealed in the Gospel, that person must learn from God's Law that he is a sinner. The wrongs must be brought to light by the Ten Commandments before they can be swallowed up by the death and resurrection of Christ, which is the climactic event of the Gospel.

Speaking practically, one must first proclaim God's Law message to convince the sinner that he has fallen short of the glory of God (Romans 3:23), that he cannot free himself from his spiritually dead condition (Ephesians 2:1), and that he must be held accountable before God's judgment throne (2 Corinthians 5:10). The sinner then sees his fault before the Lord, identifies himself as a poor, miserable sinner, and may

trust that Jesus came especially to call sinners, as a doctor treats the sick (Mark 2:17). Through the Gospel, the good news of salvation in Christ is handed to the penitent as a gift. The person hears forgiveness and so also possesses it through faith, right then and there. There is nothing more to do—not even a special prayer to pray—in order for God to show His favor and welcome back His long-lost child (see Luke 15:20).

This order of Law and Gospel presentation is seen throughout the Bible, and we notice it in the three Old Testament minor prophets we are studying: Obadiah, Jonah and Micah. Obadiah was inspired to hurl words of divine wrath against the unrepentant people of Esau. The Edomites despised their brother Israelites, so the Law of God covered them with shame and rendered the verdict that they would be cut off forever (Obadiah 10). However, this short oracle ends on a note of hope for those who by grace alone escape God's judgment and through faith in Christ become part of the Lord's kingdom. Esau's original heartfelt desire was to obtain the firstborn's blessing, but his destruction would come on "the day of the LORD" (Obadiah 15). Even though the Law pronounced that there would be no survivor for the house of Esau, the Lord provided many "saviors" who would rule in the perfect righteousness and peace that God intended (vv. 18–21).

Jonah's book ends with a question that echoes from God's mouth, "Should not I pity Nineveh?" Only in the Gospel can we see the Lord's perspective that Jonah refused to acknowledge. God took pity, and even Nineveh would revert. God chose to see the Ninevites through the perfect righteousness of Christ. This challenged the prophet that the Gospel should have the final word.

The Book of Micah hits hard right away with a harsh prophecy of judgment against both kingdoms, North and South. "Disaster has come down from the LORD to the gate of Jerusalem" (Micah 1:12), and "I will make Samaria a heap in the open country" (1:6). Yet then a brilliant promise of salvation is vividly portrayed when the prophet preaches about the coming Savior, born in Bethlehem (5:2), the ruler of a divine house that will be lifted up higher than every mountain (4:1).

In all three of these prophets, as well as in the rest of Scripture, the Law's utter condemnation is always followed by the wonderful release that is sounded out in the Gospel.

Avoid the Pitfalls

Evangelism suffers when the Good News is garbled with mankind's opinions, even when the intentions are good and results seem positive. Evangelism succeeds when Micah's invitation is followed: "Come, let us go up to the mountain of the LORD, . . . that He may teach us His ways . . . for out of Zion shall go forth the law" (Micah 4:2). The prophet's word translated "law" here actually means "instruction." It is all God's Word; that is, Law and Gospel, proclaimed in a delicate balance that must not be upset. Some errors are born out of malice or self-aggrandizement, but most missteps in evangelism are likely unintentional slips that well-meaning people, clergy or lay, stumble into. Yet we can't let our frailty prevent us from proclaiming God's Word.

Carl Ferdinand Walther put together a valuable lecture series to teach his seminary students how to avoid mistakes in distinguishing Law and Gospel. These lectures are published today as *Law and Gospel: How to Read and Apply the Bible* (CPH, 2010). Briefly speaking, if the Law is overemphasized and the Gospel downplayed, people would despair, thinking that they had no hope of receiving the Lord's favor, or they will presume that they have done enough works to earn salvation for themselves. Both of these conclusions severely injury one's faith in Christ alone. However, if the Law is treated as completely meaningless or absent, then that would turn the Gospel into a cheap spiritual amnesty that actually encourages people to sin more (cf. Romans 6:1). We still need the Law to show us the sins from which the Lord sets us free, as well as to guide us once we live under grace, conforming our lives to the pattern of Christ that has been formed in us.

Comfort the Conscience

Correcting mistakes in proclaiming Law and Gospel is an especially difficult task for both pastor and people. The risk is that we escape one extreme imbalance of Law and Gospel and fall headlong into one another—like pulling your car out of one ditch, only to slide into the other. It's better to follow the example of both the prophets and the apostles, since their aim in evangelism is constantly to maintain the balance between Law and Gospel, and then let the Gospel remain the final word to ease the sinner's conscience.

Forgiveness remains the first and highest goal in our evangelism efforts. Yet, once forgiveness has been handed out in the full sweetness of pure Gospel, we trust that God will see to it Himself that the Christian lives in better harmony with His Law. What does that look like? Micah tells us: "What does the LORD require of you but to do justice, and to love kindness, and to walk humbly with your God?" (6:8).

Isaiah and Micah

What image fills your mind when you think about an Old Testament-era prophet? A lonely man in a plain-looking robe with sandals and a walking stick? Nobody could have been lonelier than Jonah, spending three days inside a fish! Most of the time, we have only the words that the prophet recorded and not a detailed back story of the man's life.

Thankfully, most of the prophets in Scripture very carefully noted the time during which they served the Lord as His mouthpiece to Israel and the countries beyond. The most common convention was for a prophet to list the kings during whose reign he prophesied. In the era of the divided kingdom (after Solomon), the mention of kings' names give us a clue also as to whether the prophet originated in the Southern Kingdom (Judah) or the Northern (Ephraim/Israel).

Study Guide

The Ghent Altarpiece (1425–32), Hubert van Eyck, detail. Iberfoto / Iberfoto

LifeLight Expands

LifeLight

Available NOW!

The Bible: An Overview
Genesis, Pt. 1
Genesis, Pt. 2
Exodus, Pt. 1
Exodus, Pt. 2
Wilderness Wanderings
Joshua
Judges
Ruth/Esther
1 & 2 Samuel
Life of David
1 & 2 Kings
1 & 2 Chronicles

Ezra/Nehemiah
Job
Selected Psalms
Proverbs
Ecclesiastes/ Song of Solomon
Isaiah, Pt. 1
Isaiah, Pt. 2
Jeremiah/Lamentations
Ezekiel
Daniel
Hosea/Joel/Amos
Obadiah/Jonah/Micah
Minor Prophets

Nahum/Habakkuk/ Zephaniah
Haggai/Zechariah/ Malachi
Matthew, Pt. 1
Matthew, Pt. 2
Mark
Luke, Pt. 1
Luke, Pt. 2
John, Pt. 1
John, Pt. 2
Acts, Pt. 1
Acts, Pt. 2

Romans, Pt. 1
Romans, Pt. 2
1 Corinthians
2 Corinthians
Galatians/Philippians/ Colossians
Ephesians/ 1 & 2 Thessalonians
Timothy/Titus/Philemon
Hebrews
James/Jude
1 & 2 Peter
1, 2, 3 John
Revelation

LifeLight Foundations

Baptism
Bible Feasts
Creation, New Creation
The Christian's Mission

End Times
Heaven & Hell
Law & Gospel
Ministry

Miracles
Parables
Prayer

Prophecy
Triune God
Worship

LifeLight Release Schedule

2015 RELEASES

LifeLight Foundations—
Time between the Testaments — December

The Day of the Lord Is Near

Obadiah

Distribute before session 1 for use in session 1.
Use enrichment magazine pp. 2–5.

Resources for Worship

Use these resources for your daily study at home and at the week's assembly.

Hymn

Brightest and best of the stars of the morning,
Dawn on our darkness and lend us thine aid;
Star of the East, the horizon adorning,
Guide where our infant Redeemer is laid.

Shall we not yield Him, in costly devotion,
Fragrance of Edom and off'rings divine,
Gems of the mountain and pearls of the ocean,
Myrrh from the forest and gold from the mine?

Vainly we offer each ample oblation,
Vainly with gifts would His favor secure.
Richer by far is the heart's adoration;
Dearer to God are the prayers of the poor.

LSB 400:1, 3–4

Prayer

Lord God, in Your infinite wisdom and by Your almighty power, You exalt and You make small. Keep us from sinful pride and arrogance that would turn us from You, our only hope and our sure salvation. Forgive us our many sins, and renew us daily through Jesus Christ, Your Son, our Lord, who lives and reigns with You and the Holy Spirit, one God, now and forever. Amen.

Digging Deep
My Personal Study for Week 1

Day 1 • Read Genesis 25:19–34 and Jeremiah 49:7–22

1. Obadiah, whose name means "servant of the Lord [Yahweh]," records God's word against a particular nation. Write below the name of the nation and a summary of where it was located, based on a Bible atlas or a map in your Bible.

2. According to Genesis 25:19–34, what was the origin of this nation?

3. Jeremiah also writes about this nation. Read Jeremiah 49:7–22. Summarize the future of this nation.

4. The little Book of Obadiah presents some big problems for historians. There are three main suggestions about when it was written: an early date, c. 845 BC; a late date, c. 400 BC; and a date after the Babylonians destroyed Jerusalem, c. 587–555 BC. Compare Obadiah 1–4 with Jeremiah 49:14–16. What does the passage from Jeremiah suggest about the events Obadiah describes?

5. a. According to Obadiah 1, how did the prophet receive God's message about this nation?

b. What does this tell you about the nature of the prophecy?

Day 2 • Read Obadiah

Today, you will read the whole Book of Obadiah, but the questions will focus on just the first portion of the book. This is to provide a good look at the full context before studying particulars. (Reading for context will also be used for Jonah and Micah and is a good general practice for interpreters of the Bible.)

6. a. The Lord's word about the nation begins with a summons. Who is summoned?

b. Why are they summoned?

7. What reasons does the Lord give for His summons in verses 3 and 7?

8. The prophet uses some figurative language to describe what he sees happening to the nation in verses 4–9. Choose an example of this figurative language and explain what historical events it depicts.

9. Who in this nation does the Lord target for judgment?

10. How does the Lord's focused wrath speak to the circumstances of your nation today?

Day 3 • Read Obadiah 10–14 and Malachi 1:2–5

11. In Obadiah 10, the Lord states how long the punishment against the nation will last. Compare it with Malachi 1:2–5. What does this tell us about the nature of God and His judgment?

12. In Obadiah 12–14, the Lord records a series of commands against the nation ("do not . . ."). Choose two of these commands and write them as commands against sin in our day.

a. First command: Do not . . .

Arise, Go to Nineveh

Jonah 1

Distribute before session 2 for use in session 2.
Use enrichment magazine pp. 6–8.

Resources for Worship

Use these resources for your daily study at home and at the week's assembly.

Hymn

Jesus, lead Thou on
Till our rest is won;
And although the way be cheerless,
We will follow calm and fearless.
Guide us by Thy hand
To our fatherland.

If the way be drear,
If the foe be near,
Let not faithless fears o'ertake us;
Let not faith and hope forsake us;
For through many a woe
To our home we go.

When we seek relief
From a long-felt grief,
When temptations come alluring,
Make us patient and enduring.
Show us that bright shore
Where we weep no more.

Jesus, lead Thou on
Till our rest is won.
Heav'nly leader, still direct us,
Still support, console, protect us,
Till we safely stand
In our fatherland.

LSB 718

Prayer

O Lord, salvation belongs to You, and You alone! You have given us the Great Commission to preach the Gospel to all nations. How often we, like Jonah, have wanted to flee rather than to serve. Forgive us our indifference, cowardice, and prejudice. Embolden us by Your Spirit, through Jesus Christ, Your Son, our Lord, who lives and reigns with You and the Holy Spirit, one God, now and forever. Amen.

Digging Deep
My Personal Study for Week 2

Day 1 • Read 2 Kings 14:23–29

1. Apart from the Book of Jonah, 2 Kings 14 is the only other place in the Old Testament that mentions the prophet Jonah. Summarize below the setting for Jonah's ministry.

Where

What king

What circumstances

What prophecy

2. The description of the Lord in verses 24–27 provides helpful background for understanding the Book of Jonah. How does the writer of 2 Kings describe the Lord here?

3. *For personal reflection. Sharing optional.* God calls each of us to share His Word—both the harsh message of the Law and the life-giving message of the Gospel—with those around us. How does the ministry of Jonah in 2 Kings 14 encourage you to share God's Word today?

Day 2 • Read Jonah 1

4. The name Jonah means "dove" or "pigeon" in Hebrew. According to Leviticus 1:14–17, what special roles did doves have in Hebrew culture?

5. Jonah's father's name, Amittai, means "faithful" or "loyal." What irony do you see between the name of Jonah's father and Jonah's actions in 1:3?

6. Twice in verse 3, Jonah is said to flee "from the presence of the LORD" (literally, from "the face of the LORD"). Based on Genesis 3:8 and 4:16, what is the state of Jonah's mind and heart?

7. Israel sought the presence of the Lord at the tabernacle or temple, where God promised to be present to bless His people. How do believers today seek the Lord's presence?

8. *For personal reflection. Sharing optional.* What special requests would you make of the Lord in His presence?

Day 3 • Read Jonah 1:4–6

9. **Challenge question**. These few verses of Jonah raise some challenging theological questions. Based on Jonah 1:4 and Job 1:12–19 (especially vv. 16, 18–19), is God responsible for all "natural" disasters? Why or why not?

10. Are God's actions fair toward the sailors who suffer damage to their ship and who lose their cargo? Why or why not?

Jonah's Prayer and Preaching

Jonah 2–3

Distribute before session 3 for use in session 3.
Use enrichment magazine pp. 9–11.

Resources for Worship

Use these resources for your daily study at home and at the week's assembly.

Hymn

I lay my sins on Jesus,
The spotless Lamb of God;
He bears them all and frees us
From the accursèd load.
I bring my guilt to Jesus
To wash my crimson stains
Clean in His blood most precious
Till not a spot remains.

I lay my wants on Jesus;
All fullness dwells in Him;
He heals all my diseases;
My soul He does redeem.
I lay my griefs on Jesus,
My burdens and my cares;
He from them all releases;
He all my sorrows shares.

I rest my soul on Jesus,
This weary soul of mine;
His right hand me embraces;
I on His breast recline.
I love the name of Jesus,
Immanuel, Christ, the Lord;
Like fragrance on the breezes
His name abroad is poured.

LSB 606

Prayer

O Lord our God, in our distress, we have called to You, and You have heard and answered us. Thank You for preserving our life through many dangers and for keeping us in the saving faith. Be with us until life's end, when we shall rise from death to life eternal, through Jesus, Your Son, our Lord, who lives and reigns with You and the Holy Spirit, one God, now and forever. Amen.

Digging Deep
My Personal Study for Week 3

Day 1 • Read Jonah 1:17–2:9

1. How does Jonah 1:17 reveal the mercy of God?

2. Many accounts of Jonah's story refer to the creature that swallowed him as a whale (e.g., the ancient Jewish historian Josephus). English translations, based on the Hebrew, consistently say it was a great "fish." Does it matter which way we tell the story? Why or why not?

3. *For personal reflection. Sharing optional.* How does Jonah's prayer challenge and inspire you to pray in difficult circumstances?

Challenge

Inspire

4. In verse 2, Jonah used a particular word to describe the creature. What does this word mean? (See Psalm 49:13–15; 89:48 for help.)

5. In 1:9, Jonah made an important confession about who the Lord is. According to 2:2, what further truths about the Lord does Jonah learn and confess?

Day 2 • Read Jonah 2:3–4 and 2 Chronicles 7:11–16

6. a. In 2:3, Jonah describes the experience of plunging into the stormy sea. From Jonah's perspective, who hurled him into the water (cf. 1:15)?

b. To whom do the waves belong?

c. What point is Jonah trying to make with his wording?

7. How does 2:4 dramatically express the depth of Jonah's faith?

8. Based on 2 Chronicles 7:11–16, what is the state of Jonah's heart?

Day 3 • Read Jonah 2:5–10

9. What is the "land" or "pit" in verse 6?

10. Based on what the poem says in verses 2–7, did Jonah die?

11. In Matthew 12:38–41, Jesus applies the story of Jonah for scribes and Pharisees. According to Jesus, what did the story of Jonah prophesy?

Should Not I Pity Nineveh?

Jonah 4

Distribute before session 4 for use in session 4.
Use enrichment magazine pp. 12–15.

Resources for Worship

Use these resources for your daily study at home and at the week's assembly.

Hymn

Hark, the voice of Jesus calling,
"Who will go and work today?
Fields are white and harvests waiting—
Who will bear the sheaves away?"
Loud and long the Master calleth;
Rich reward He offers thee.
Who will answer, gladly saying,
"Here am I, send me, send me"?

Some take up His task in morning,
To their Lord responding soon;
Some are called in heat of midday,
Others late in afternoon;
Even as the sun is setting,
Some are sent into the fields,
There to gather in the bounty
That God's Word so richly yields.

For as rain and snow from heaven
Water seeds in dusty soil,
Causing them to bud and flower,
Giving bread to those who toil;
So the Lord sends forth His promise,
Words of life and joy and peace—
Never void to Him returning,
Bearing fruit with great increase.

Hearken to the Lord whose coming
Marks the time when grace shall end,
When with His angelic reapers
He in glory shall descend.
Soon the night, the final harvest;
Soon the time for work shall cease.
Then the souls His grace has garnered
Shall enjoy His Sabbath peace.

LSB 827

Prayer

O God, in pity, You reach out to this fallen world. You have graciously brought us to faith in Your Son, our Savior. Forgive us for the times when, rather than sharing this Gospel, we have kept it from others. Enable us to reflect Your love toward all people, through Jesus Christ, Your Son, our Lord, who lives and reigns with You and the Holy Spirit, one God, now and forever. Amen.

Digging Deep
My Personal Study for Week 4

Day 1 • Read Jonah 4

1. What? After preaching such an effective sermon, the preacher is angry! Why is Jonah angry?

2. What detail about the events described earlier do we learn in verse 2?

3. The words of Jonah 4:2b are known as "the John 3:16 of the Old Testament" because they are so loved by Old Testament writers (repeated about eight times). Read Exodus 32:1–4; 34:1. What disastrous events in Israel's history led God to first speak these famous words in Exodus 34:6–7?

4. How had the Lord fulfilled each of these divine attributes in Jonah's life?

Gracious God and merciful

Slow to anger

Abounding in steadfast love

Relenting from disaster

Day 2 • Read Jonah 4:3–4

5. Contrast the way Moses prays in Exodus 32:30–32 with the way Jonah prays in Jonah 4:3.

6. In view of Moses, what prayer should Jonah be praying?

7. *For personal reflection. Sharing optional.* Relate the words of Jonah 4:2 to your own life. How do you see the Lord fulfilling each of these divine attributes for the good of your life?

Gracious God and merciful

Slow to anger

Abounding in steadfast love

Relenting from disaster

Day 3 • Read Jonah 4:5–6

8. What is Jonah up to in verse 5?

9. Earlier, we read that the Lord "appointed a great fish to swallow up Jonah" (1:17). Now the Lord makes a new appointment: a plant. Why?

The Lord Is Coming

Micah 1

Distribute before session 5 for use in session 5.
Use enrichment magazine pp. 16–19.

Resources for Worship

Use these resources for your daily study at home and at the week's assembly.

Hymn

God moves in a mysterious way
His wonders to perform;
He plants His footsteps in the sea
And rides upon the storm.

Judge not the Lord by feeble sense,
But trust Him for His grace;
Behind a frowning providence
Faith sees a smiling face.

His purposes will ripen fast,
Unfolding ev'ry hour;
The bud may have a bitter taste,
But sweet will be the flow'r.

Blind unbelief is sure to err
And scan His work in vain;
God is His own interpreter,
And He will make it plain.

You fearful saints, fresh courage take;
The clouds you so much dread
Are big with mercy and will break
In blessings on your head.

LSB 765

Prayer

O Lord, beneath whom the mountains melt and the valleys are split, how awesome is Your power, how terrible Your judgments! Because of our sins, we deserve nothing but punishment both now and forever. Forgive us, and strengthen our faith, as we cling to Your promises of mercy, through Jesus Christ, Your Son, our Lord, who lives and reigns with You and the Holy Spirit, one God, now and forever. Amen.

Digging Deep
My Personal Study for Week 5

Day 1 • Read Micah 1; 2 Chronicles 27:1–28:4; 28:22–29:2

1. Micah begins his prophecy by noting the kings who reigned during his ministry. Based on the readings from 2 Chronicles, summarize the conditions in Judah during the reign of each king:

Jotham

Ahaz

Hezekiah

2. If Micah served from only the last year of Jotham and the first year of Hezekiah, his ministry would have spanned at least twenty-two years. If he served from the beginning of Jotham's reign to the end of Hezekiah's, his ministry would have spanned more than sixty years. In view of what happened during the reign of Ahaz, what do these basic facts tell us about the prophet?

3. Compare Micah 1:1 with Isaiah 1:1. What conclusions can you draw about the prophet Micah based on the differences in the opening words of these two prophets?

Day 2 • Read Micah 1:2–5a

4. Micah 1:1 told us the focus of Micah's ministry. But according to verses 2–3, what is the full scope of his prophecy? (See also Micah 5:4.)

5. Micah compares a coming event to both fire and water (v. 4). What event does God show him for the beginning of his prophecy?

6. Why is this event taking place?

7. In the Old Testament, the temple was known as a place of sacrifices for giving thanks to God and as a place of atonement for sin. How is the new role described in verse 2 different from these earlier roles for the temple?

8. Although Micah summons the attention of the whole earth, the events he has in mind are local. In view of 2 Kings 17:6 and 25:1–7, what events fulfilled Micah's opening prophecy?

Against Samaria

Against Jerusalem

Day 3 • Read Micah 1:5b–7

9. Micah writes that "the transgression of Jacob" is "Samaria." How is Samaria a fitting explanation for the transgression? (See 1 Kings 16:23–26 for help.)

Gather the Remnant

Micah 2–3

Distribute before session 6 for use in session 6.
Use enrichment magazine pp. 20–22.

Resources for Worship

Use these resources for your daily study at home and at the week's assembly.

Hymn

Have no fear, little flock;
Have no fear, little flock,
  For the Father has chosen
  To give you the Kingdom;
Have no fear, little flock!

Have good cheer, little flock;
Have good cheer, little flock,
  For the Father will keep you
  In His love forever;
Have good cheer, little flock!

Praise the Lord high above;
Praise the Lord high above,
  For He stoops down to heal you,
  Uplift and restore you;
Praise the Lord high above!

Thankful hearts raise to God;
Thankful hearts raise to God,
  For He stays close beside you,
  In all things works with you;
Thankful hearts raise to God!

LSB 735;

Prayer

Almighty Father, how the world's high and mighty despise the preaching of Your Word and those who bring it! Yet You protect and gather the remnant of Your people. In these increasingly godless times, keep us in Your Word, and use us to share Your grace with a dying world, through Jesus, Your Son, our Lord, who lives and reigns with You and the Holy Spirit, one God, now and forever. Amen.

Digging Deep
My Personal Study for Week 6

Day 1 • Read Micah 2:1–5

1. Just as Micah 1 began with judgment, so does the second chapter. What societal crime does the prophet address in these opening verses?

2. a. Life in Israel was based on principles of inheritance, which bound people to their history and provided for their future. Scan Joshua 21. How did Israel receive its inheritance?

b. What truths did Israel's inheritance teach them?

3. Micah 2:3 literally says, "Against this family I am devising evil, . . . for it will be a time of evil." Typically, we do not think of the Lord as "devising evil." How do the decisions of the translators help us sort through this issue to clearly understand what the Lord is up to?

4. How does the title for Israel here ("family") reflect the Lord's will for the Israelites as they handle matters of inheritance?

Day 2 • Read Micah 2:6–13

5. a. What admonition does Israel have for the prophet?

b. What sermon would they rather hear?

6. What affect does God long to provide through His Word? (See v. 7b.)

7. In verses 12–13, Micah finally reaches his hopeful message for the people. Yet it is also touched with sadness. Note each element below.

Sad elements

Hopeful elements

8. What do these elements teach about the lives of Christians?

9. In verse 10, Micah tells the people they must "arise and go" because their land has become no place to rest and is unclean. Yet he also shortly describes a beautiful image of how the Lord will provide for their new life (v. 12c). What comfort do you find in this imagery?

Day 3 • Read Micah 3:1–4

10. a. What fundamental problem plagues Israel (v. 2a)?

b. Why does this fundamental problem arise?

Walk in the Name of the Lord

Micah 4–5

Distribute before session 7 for use in session 7.
Use enrichment magazine pp. 23–25.

Resources for Worship

Use these resources for your daily study at home and at the week's assembly.

Hymn

"Come, follow Me," the Savior spake,
"All in My way abiding;
Deny yourselves, the world forsake,
Obey My call and guiding.
O bear the cross, whate'er betide,
Take My example for your guide.

"I am the light, I light the way,
A godly life displaying;
I bid you walk as in the day;
I keep your feet from straying.
I am the way, and well I show
How you must sojourn here below.

"My heart abounds in lowliness,
My soul with love is glowing;
And gracious words My lips express,
With meekness overflowing.
My heart, My mind, My strength, My all,
To God I yield, on Him I call.

"I teach you how to shun and flee
What harms your soul's salvation,
Your heart from ev'ry guile to free,
From sin and its temptation.
I am the refuge of the soul
And lead you to your heav'nly goal."

Then let us follow Christ, our Lord,
And take the cross appointed
And, firmly clinging to His Word,
In suff'ring be undaunted.
For those who bear the battle's strain
The crown of heav'nly life obtain.

LSB 688

Prayer

In keeping with Your promise, O Lord, from the little town of Bethlehem, the Ruler of Israel and of all creation has come forth. May the ends of the earth turn to Him and live! Uplift us by the certainty of Your Word, and strengthen our faith in our Savior, Jesus Christ, Your Son, our Lord, who lives and reigns with You and the Holy Spirit, one God, now and forever. Amen.

Digging Deep
My Personal Study for Week 7

Day 1 • Read Micah 4

1. a. Zion, a name for the temple mount in Jerusalem, will be changed in the latter days. How will it be different?

b. What is the cause of this transformation?

2. **Challenge question**. In 1959, Soviet sculptor Evgeniy Vuchetich created "Let Us Beat Swords into Plowshares." His homeland, the Soviet Union, donated the sculpture to the United Nations. The sculpture portrayed the end of war. How is Micah's earlier use of these words (vv. 3–4) different from the modern political use of them?

3. How does one "walk in the name of the LORD" (v. 5)? (See Genesis 17:1–2; Judges 2:20–22; Proverbs 8:20.)

4. When will Micah's vision for Zion be fulfilled?

Day 2 • Read Micah 4:6–8

5. Jesus' ministry of healing the lame in Galilee and Judea is famous, and perhaps the first thing one may think of when reading this prophecy. Yet what does Micah write to make clear that his prophecy was not focused on or limited to Jesus' earthly ministry?

6. Does God afflict believers? Explain your answer.

7. "Remnant" (v. 7) is a favorite term in the Prophets, and could express God's wrath or His favor. How does Micah use the expression in this case?

8. a. In verse 8, how does Micah envision the future of Zion?

b. How will the Lord fulfill this vision in our lives?

Day 3 • Read Micah 4:9–13

9. How would you reply to Micah's question, "Is there no king in you [Judah]?" Explain your answer.

Walk Humbly with Your God

Micah 6

Distribute before session 8 for use in session 8.
Use enrichment magazine pp. 26–28.

Resources for Worship

Use these resources for your daily study at home and at the week's assembly.

Hymn

May we Thy precepts, Lord, fulfill
And do on earth our Father's will
    As angels do above;
Still walk in Christ, the living way,
With all Thy children and obey
    The law of Christian love.

So may we join Thy name to bless,
Thy grace adore, Thy pow'r confess,
    From sin and strife to flee.
One is our calling, one our name,
The end of all our hopes the same,
    A crown of life with Thee.

Spirit of life, of love and peace,
Unite our hearts, our joy increase,
    Thy gracious help supply.
To each of us the blessing give
In Christian fellowship to live,
    In joyful hope to die.

LSB 698

Prayer

O Lord God almighty, we bow before You in worship, thankful for Your countless gifts of grace. Forgive our sins, renew us, strengthen us, and guide us so that we may daily serve You by doing justice, loving kindness, and walking humbly with You. We ask this through Jesus Christ, Your Son, our Lord, who lives and reigns with You and the Holy Spirit, one God, now and forever. Amen.

Digging Deep
My Personal Study for Week 8

Day 1 • Read Micah 6

1. In Deuteronomy 6:4–9, Moses famously appealed to Israel in what became known as the *Shema*, from the Hebrew word for "hear." What does this creedlike statement declare?

2. a. In verse 1, Micah introduces a different appeal. To whom does the prophet address this new appeal?

b. What is the purpose of an indictment?

3. Who is to witness the testimony and pass judgment?

4. The witnesses Micah describes are mentioned earlier in the Scripture. Read Leviticus 18:24–30; 20:22–26. What causes the witnesses to pass judgment?

Day 2 • Read Micah 6:3–5

5. The Lord asks, "O My people, what have I done to you?" Write below an answer to the Lord's question.

6. The Lord also asks, "How have I wearied you?" What does this question imply about Israel's state of mind?

7. The Lord's comment in verse 4a is reminiscent of a famous earlier text in the Bible. Read Exodus 20:1–17. What does God have in mind as He addresses His people?

8. What did Balak devise, according to Numbers 22:1–6?

9. How was the Lord's will revealed in Balaam's answers, such as Numbers 23:7–10; 24:15–19?

Day 3 • Read Micah 6:6–8

10. The Lord's indictment and declarations of how He rescued Israel cause the prophet to ask questions. What is the goal of his questions?

11. For the prophet, coming "before the LORD" has a very specific location. What clues in verses 6–7 help to explain where to come "before the LORD"?

When I Fall, I Shall Rise

Micah 7

Distribute before session 9 for use in session 9.
Use enrichment magazine pp. 29–32.

Resources for Worship

Use these resources for your daily study at home and at the week's assembly.

Hymn

Rise! To arms! With prayer employ you,
O Christians, lest the foe destroy you;
For Satan has designed your fall.
Wield God's Word, the weapon glorious;
Against all foes be thus victorious,
For God protects you from them all.
Fear not the hordes of hell,
Here is Emmanuel.
Hail the Savior!
The strong foes yield
To Christ, our shield,
And we, the victors, hold the field.

Cast afar this world's vain pleasure
And boldly strive for heav'nly treasure.
Be steadfast in the Savior's might.
Trust the Lord, who stands beside you,
For Jesus from all harm will hide you.
By faith you conquer in the fight.
Take courage, weary soul!
Look forward to the goal!
Joy awaits you.
The race well run,
Your long war won,
Your crown shines splendid as the sun.

Wisely fight, for time is fleeting;
The hours of grace are fast retreating;
Short, short is this our earthly way.
When the Lord the dead will waken
And sinners all by fear are shaken,
The saints with joy will greet that day.
Praise God, our triumph's sure.
We need not long endure
Scorn and trial.
Our Savior King
His own will bring
To that great glory which we sing.

LSB 668

Prayer

Who is a God like You, O Lord, pardoning iniquity and passing over transgression? Our hearts overflow with joy as we consider Your compassion, faithfulness, and steadfast love! Be with us now and throughout this life, until we join the saints in heaven above to praise You, through Jesus Christ, Your Son, our Lord, who lives and reigns with You and the Holy Spirit, one God, now and forever. Amen.

Digging Deep
My Personal Study for Week 9

Day 1 • Read Micah 7

1. In verse 1, Micah refers to a harvest law among the Israelites. Read Deuteronomy 24:19–22. What was the law and its purpose?

Law

Purpose

2. What does Micah's declaration in 7:2 mean for our life and salvation? (Cf. Romans 3:10–20.)

3. Micah 7:3 says that leaders of the community "weave it together." What is the purpose of their weaving?

4. Read Jotham's parable of the bramble in Judges 9:7–15, and write below how Micah's rebuke in 7:4a shames the leaders of Israel and Judah.

5. Read John 19:2–5 and Hebrews 10:19–23. How did the thorns Christ wore contribute to our salvation?

Day 2 • Read Micah 7:4b–7

6. Based on Ezekiel 33:7–9, what would be "your watchmen . . . your punishment" that Micah describes?

7. In 7:5–6, Micah describes a shocking circumstance. What will "The day . . . of your punishment" be like?

8. What confident example does the prophet offer to those who hear his harsh message about that day?

9. a. In Micah 7:7, the prophet describes his patience and refers to his action. What is the prophet doing?

b. How would you put these actions to use in your own life when trying circumstances surround you?

Day 3 • Read Micah 7:8–13

10. This portion of Micah includes one of the book's greatest statements of faith and hope. Micah's words are not a boast but an example of a believer's confidence. Read verse 8. In view of Micah's declaration, how would you express your confidence in the Lord?

11. a. In verse 9, what somber reality tempers the prophet's bold statement?

b. How does the Lord assist him?

12. In verses 6, 8, and 10, the prophet mentions his enemies. The word *enemy* occurs in different forms. It likely refers to the rebellious people of Israel (v. 6, masculine plural) as well as the whole earth that taunts God's people (vv. 8, 10, 13, feminine singular; *earth* is feminine in Hebrew). Who are the enemies of God's people today?

13. a. What shining promise does Micah prophesy for the future of God's people in verses 11–12?

b. How is this fulfilled?

Day 4 • Read Micah 7:14–17

14. For what is the prophet praying in verse 14?

15. a. Consult a map in your Bible. Where are the regions of Bashan and Gilead?

b. According to 2 Kings 10:32–33 and 15:29, what had become of these regions in Micah's day?

16. a. How will the nations see no evil, speak no evil, and hear no evil (vv. 16–17)?

b. What will cause this transformation (vv. 15; 17c)?

Day 5 • Read Micah 7:18–20

17. Micah's name means "Who is like the Lord?" and he pays tribute to that name in verse 18. What "marvelous things" (v. 15) top the prophet's list when describing the Lord?

18. Micah's wording in verses 18b–19a returns to the "John 3:16 of the Old Testament," the Lord's declaration of Himself in Exodus 34:6–7. How does the Exodus passage focus both the wrath of God and His mercy on human beings?

19. *For personal reflection. Sharing optional.* Think of the sins that trouble you most—past and present. How does the imagery in Micah 7:19 comfort you in the face of your struggles?

20. **Challenge question**. Micah ends his prophecy with a confident appeal to the covenant promises that God extended to Abraham, Isaac, and Jacob. Some of these promises were concluded in the Old Testament, but some of them continue to apply to us today. Read Genesis 12:1–3; 26:2–5; 28:13–15.

a. Which promises to the patriarchs applied only then?

b. Which promises still apply to us today?

12. How does the title "God on high" reveal a deeper sense of what it means to be "before the LORD"?

13. The answer to the prophet's questions in verses 6–7 is obviously "No." What does the Lord really want?

14. *For personal reflection. Sharing optional.* In verse 8, the prophet is not teaching a series of works by which we may redeem or save ourselves, since it is the Lord who redeems and saves (vv. 4–5). He describes acts that are fitting for the redeemed. In what ways do these actions show God's gracious favor and salvation in your life as a believer?

Do justice

Love kindness

Walk humbly with your God

Day 4 • Read Micah 6:9–15

15. What works of injustice, unkindness, and arrogance does the prophet decry?

16. The Lord introduces another appeal with the word "Hear!" Why would this new set of indictments be cried in the city rather than the country?

17. In verses 13–15, the Lord describes a coming desolation. What does the wording reveal about how this desolation will take place?

18. What resource does the Lord offer as His means to deliver the people?

19. Read Proverbs 8:22–31 and John 1:1–5. What prayer of thanks to the Lord would you offer for this resource?

Day 5 • Read Micah 6:16

20. Read 1 Kings 16:25–26. What were the "statutes of Omri"?

21. According to 1 Kings 16:31–33, what other works were added by the "house of Ahab"?

22. Omri and his son Ahab were rulers in the Northern Kingdom of Israel at Samaria. How did their "statutes" and "works" influence the Southern Kingdom of Judah? Read 2 Chronicles 18:1–3; 19:1–3.

23. According to Micah 6:16, for what ominous reason did the Lord allow Samaria's influence to reach Judah?

24. Some animals hiss when they are angry, and the ancient Israelites apparently had a way of mimicking these sounds to express their scorn. In fact, in Jewish tradition, the congregation would hiss during the reading of the Book of Esther whenever the villain of that story was mentioned (Haman the Agagite). If hissing is the appropriate sound for scorn, what sounds should God's people express for justice, kindness, and humility? (See Micah 6:8; read Esther 9:19, 22 for ideas.)

10. In verses 9–10, Micah describes Judah's coming exile with a familiar biblical illustration of overwhelming difficulties: labor pains. In verse 11, he uses a more violent comparison to describe the exile. How are these comparisons fitting for what the exiled people would experience?

11. What is it that the nations do not understand as they gather about Zion?

12. What will happen to the wealth of the nations?

13. Micah foresaw the exile of Judah one hundred or more years before it took place in 587 BC. He closes this portion of his prophecy in proclamation to "the Lord of the whole earth" (v. 13). How does this title for the Lord and Micah's earlier prophecy about the nations (vv. 1b–2) provide hope to Judah and to you?

Day 4 • Read Micah 5:1–6

14. In verse 1, the prophet uses some unique expressions. Based on the prophet's earlier statements, what is meant by the following expressions? (For help, see 4:8–10, 13.)

Daughter of troops

Judge of Israel

15. a. Verse 2 is a prophecy cited also in the New Testament (Matthew 2:6). How does the Lord fulfill this prophecy about a ruler?

b. In view of the New Testament fulfillment, what does Micah teach with the words "whose coming forth is from of old, from ancient days"?

16. Who is "she" and "His brothers" in verse 3?

17. The statement in verses 5b–6 appears to be a boast of Judeans who would apply Micah's prophecy of the "ruler" (v. 2) to their own time. According to 2 Chronicles 32:20–23, how did the Lord deliver Judah from the Assyrians?

Day 5 • Read Micah 5:7–15

18. The Judeans' boast of conquest will not be fulfilled. Instead, the Lord ultimately intends exile for His people. In verses 7–9, the Lord describes different experiences of His people in exile. Describe and contrast them.

Verse 7

Verses 8–9

19. The Book of Esther describes a specific fulfillment of the prophecy given in Micah 5:8–9. Read Esther 8:15–9:3. How did the Lord fulfill the prophecy of Micah in this case?

20. a. Read together Micah 4:1–4 and 5:10–15. What will the Lord provide "in that day"?

b. What will He take away?

21. *For personal reflection. Sharing optional.* Each of us lives in view of "that day" when the Lord will accomplish His will fully among us. However, in preparation for that day, what does the Lord provide for your good now? What will He take away?

The Lord provides

The Lord will take away

11. Micah uses hideous imagery to describe the depravity of the leaders in Israel. What practices would this imagery describe? (For a clue, read Galatians 5:13–15.)

12. In verse 4, Micah has a specific future event in mind that will happen "then . . . at that time," which he already described in chapter 2. What event is the prophet anticipating as he observes the evil deeds of Israel?

13. Verse 1 raises an important question in the whole of Micah's prophecy: "Is it not for you to know justice?" How does one know justice?

Before God

Before others

Day 4 • Read Micah 3:5–8

14. a. What sort of people are the false prophets that Micah renounces?

b. How can Micah's observation help us identify false prophets today?

15. a. What do the prophets stand to lose because of their sins?

b. How might this serve as a warning to believers today?

16. a. Note well the confidence Micah describes as he prophesies. What resources does he enjoy as a true prophet of the Lord?

b. *For personal reflection. Sharing optional.* In view of the challenges in life that you now face, which of these resources would you most request from the Lord? Explain your answer.

Day 5 • Read Micah 3:9–12

17. In these verses, Micah specifically talks about problems not just in Israel generally but especially at Zion and Jerusalem. These verses are a crescendo for Micah's opening chapters of judgment. What makes his indictment against Zion and Jerusalem such a climax?

18. a. With a threefold flourish, Micah identifies the true desire of the leaders in Israel. What do they want?

b. Why is this no surprise for us today?

19. Is it wrong to "lean on the LORD" (v. 11)? Why or why not?

20. Compare the words of the leaders in Jerusalem in verse 11b and Paul's words in 2 Timothy 4:18. How are they different?

10. a. In Hebrew, "high place" has an obvious meaning (as in v. 3) and a less obvious meaning. Read 2 Chronicles 28:25. What else does "high place" describe?

b. Based on your answer, what has the Lord shown the prophet about Jerusalem, home to the Lord's temple? (See 2 Chronicles 28:22–25.)

11. Archaeology has revealed the gifts of King Omri of Israel as an administrator and as a builder who erected a palace at Samaria, which became the splendid new capital for the Northern Kingdom of Israel. How does the Lord see Samaria, based on 1:6?

12. How had Samaria grown so prosperous?

Day 4 • Read Micah 1:8–9

13. a. In verses 6–7, the Lord is speaking. Who is the speaker in verses 8–9?

b. How do these verses justify your answer?

14. Compare Micah 1:8 with Isaiah 20:2–5 and write below what the actions mean in each case.

Micah 1:8

Isaiah 20:2–5

15. What is the incurable wound that has reached Judah?

Day 5 • Read Micah 1:10–16

16. a. "Tell it not in Gath" was a famous declaration in Israel. What should not be told? (See 2 Samuel 1:17–27.)

b. How does this relate to the events Micah foresees in verses 10–16?

17. In verses 10, 11, 12, 14, and 15, the prophet puns on the names of towns in Judah. Beth-le-aphrah means "house of dust," Shaphir means "beautiful"; all the names have similar points of irony. What overall point does the prophet drive toward as he plays on these words?

18. Pointing out irony is a common feature of humor. Is there a place for such humor in the somber messages of the church today? Explain your answer.

19. a. The first chapter of Micah is a thoroughgoing proclamation of disaster and of God's judgment. Micah offers no consolation. Yet the prophet's name literally means "Who is like the Lord?" What consolation for Micah and his people do you see in the prophet's name?

b. What consolation might you take for yourself from the prophet's name?

10. **Challenge question**. Jonah 4:6 contains a key word found a total of ten times throughout the story, which is commonly translated as "discomfort" here. Compare the following passages to discover the word's basic meaning and to consider its significance at this moment in Jonah's life: 1:2, 7, 8; 3:8.

Basic meaning

How the word describes Jonah's standing before the Lord

Day 4 • Read Jonah 4:7–8

11. God makes two more appointments. What purposes do these appointments serve?

12. How would you characterize Jonah's state of mind in 4:8?

13. Earlier, we considered why God appointed the plant for Jonah (4:6; question 9). How do the events of 4:7–8 more fully reveal God's purposes?

14. Apply these events of Jonah's life for believers today. How do they illustrate God's work?

15. Read Job 1:21. What can you learn from Job's comments about the circumstances of life as we experience them?

Day 5 • Read Jonah 4:9–11

16. According to the Lord, why does Jonah not have a reason to feel angry about the death of the plant?

17. a. Jonah 4 is dominated by questions and even ends with a question. What answer does the Lord intend for His final question (v. 11)?

b. What evidence from the Book of Jonah can you cite to back up your answer?

18. A common question people ask is why some people receive God's salvation and others do not. How do the descriptions of the Lord in the Book of Jonah help us answer this question?

19. How has your study of the Book of Jonah encouraged you to share God's Word with others or to support mission work?

12. In verse 8, Jonah speaks of "hope of steadfast love." Yet the rest of the verse describes conditions that deprive people of such love, admonishing believers to single-hearted devotion. How does one abide in God's steadfast love?

13. Jonah 2:7 says that the prophet "remembered the LORD." What practices do the contents of verses 7 and 9 encourage you to use when you pray?

Day 4 • Read Jonah 3

14. In what ways does the Book of Jonah describe Nineveh?

15. Jonah preached an effective message. What is the summary of Jonah's message?

16. How did the people of Nineveh show that they believed Jonah's message?

17. *For personal reflection. Sharing optional.* Recall a time when God used your words to touch someone else's life. As time and willingness permit, relate your story to others in the group.

What I said

What it did

18. *For personal reflection. Sharing optional.* The example of Jonah's preaching reveals just how effective God's Word can be in people's lives. In view of Jonah's example of Hebrews 4:12, write below the name of someone you know who could benefit from hearing God's Word from you. Then write what you might say to that person.

Name

What I would say

Day 5 • Read Jonah 3:6–10

19. In 3:5, we read that the people of Nineveh, from greatest to least, responded to God's Word. Now verses 6–7 tell us how the king himself responded. What did the king do?

20. a. Reflect on the king's order in verses 7–8. What would naturally happen from such practices?

b. How might this help the people of Nineveh?

21. What outcome did the king hope for (v. 9)?

22. What does the Scripture mean when it says that the Lord "relented" (v. 10)?

11. To the ship's captain, Jonah's God is just one god among many who might hear their prayers. Based on Hebrews 11:6, does God hear the prayers of those who pray as the sailors do here?

Day 4 • Read Jonah 1:7–10

12. What does it mean to "cast lots"?

13. The sailors spray Jonah with a stream of questions, revealing their desperation for an answer. What question(s) did Jonah leave unanswered in his reply of verse 9?

14. Jonah states "I fear the LORD." What does it mean to "fear" the Lord? (Read Psalm 119:38; 130:4 for help.)

15. People who worship many gods typically have a god for each major natural phenomenon. How does Jonah's confession show that his God is different?

16. Jonah told the sailors that he was "fleeing from the presence of the LORD" (1:10). How does Jonah's confession of his actions conflict with his confession of the Lord in verse 9?

Day 5 • Read Jonah 1:11–16

17. Jonah stuns us with his answer to the sailors' question in verse 11. Is Jonah's answer a statement of faith or a statement of despair? Explain your answer.

18. What fear do the sailors express in verse 14?

19. *For personal reflection. Sharing optional.* Four times, the sailors speak of prayer or seeking God's will in the midst of their hardship (vv. 6, 7, 14, and 16). In contrast, chapter 1 records no prayers from Jonah! How do you respond when you face hardship?

20. In question 14, we explored what it means to "fear" the Lord. Apply what you learned to the description of the sailors in verse 16. What does this verse tell us and not tell us about their "fear"?

Tells us

Does not tell us

b. Second command: Do not . . .

13. Now turn these negative commands into something positive that the Lord calls His people to do for others.

a. First positive command: Do . . .

b. Second positive command: Do . . .

14. Why was it so important for the Lord to love, protect, and preserve the people of Judah? (Read Matthew 2:1–6, if you need help.)

Day 4 • Read Obadiah 15–18

15. So far the passages of Obadiah have focused on God's wrath and judgment on a particular nation. How do these verses introduce changes of focus?

16. What principle of justice does the Lord apply to the nations?

17. In verse 17, the Lord speaks a promise in connection with Zion, where the temple and its covenant services were held. What will become of Zion?

18. How does the Lord transform the house of Jacob and of Joseph?

19. Today, there is no "house of Esau," as the Lord said would happen. Its inhabitants were certainly overwhelmed by judgment. But according to Deuteronomy 23:7–8; Amos 9:12; and Mark 3:7–8, how else might the house of Esau (Idumea) disappear?

Day 5 • Read Obadiah 19–21

20. In these verses, the Lord gives a geography lesson and also declares the future of His people. How do the tribal names Ephraim and Benjamin help explain who "those of the Negeb" and "those of the Shephelah" are? (If you need further clues, read 1 Chronicles 9:1–3.)

21. We don't usually see the word "Savior" in the plural as "saviors." According to Judges 3:9, what kind of persons are such "saviors"?

22. According to verse 21, who will be the ultimate Savior?

23. **Challenge question**. Obadiah prophesied that "the kingdom shall be the LORD's." According to Matthew 6:10, is the prophecy of Obadiah fulfilled? Explain why or why not.

Considering the vast Old Testament span of history, it is the exception, rather than the rule, that two writing prophets would live in the same region and prophesy at the same time. Yet that is what we have with the prophets Isaiah and Micah. How could they not have interacted? Where one would leave off, the other could pick up the divine message afresh. Were they ever preaching in the same place, or could they have been persecuted in the same way? Or did both Isaiah and Micah follow the stereotype of the lonely prophet and stick to themselves and their own work, uttering prophecies in their own respective bases of operation? In support of the possibility that they worked together, we have significant similarities and distinctions to explore as we keep in mind these two contemporary men of God.

City versus Country

Not only did Isaiah and Micah live and preach during the same time period, but they also were residents of the same region—Judah. Isaiah was inspired to write a much larger work than Micah, but his subject matter was especially directed specifically to the city of Jerusalem and the rest of Judah surrounding the capital (Isaiah 1:1; 2:1). Micah, on the other hand, wrote a shorter book (hence the designation as a Minor Prophet) but was called by the Lord to preach words not only about Jerusalem but also about Samaria (Micah 1:1), the capital city of the Northern Kingdom of Israel and home of the evil, idolatrous kings that followed the rebellious King Jeroboam.

Thanks to the historical passages that Isaiah narrates, it is easy to perceive that he was closely involved with the daily, even personal, affairs of the kings who reigned in Jerusalem. King Hezekiah especially sought the prophet's advice, and received comfort from him that he would recover from a life-threatening illness (Isaiah 37 and 38; 2 Kings 19 and 20). He apparently enjoyed frequent access to the temple, but whether that means he was a priest, a privileged servant, or simply a frequent worshiper, cannot be pinned down for certain.

In contrast, Micah wrote poetic, divine utterances without very much context or historical information included. We don't know how Micah's original audience received his message, nor what became of him at the end of his ministry. It is supposed from Jewish legend (since the Bible doesn't explicitly say it) that Isaiah was one of the faithful saints listed as suffering martyrdom by being "sawn in two" in Hebrews 11:37. But with Micah, it is impossible even to guess the circumstances of his death.

We are privileged to know, however, that Micah's hometown was the little town of Moresheth. Sometimes the village's name is lengthened to Moresheth-gath, presumably to indicate the larger and more prominent Philistine city close by. Several other local towns also earn a mention from this rural prophet: Lachish, Achzib, Zaanan, Shaphir and Adullam (ch. 1). A little more than a day's journey away from Jerusalem, Moresheth had certainly more of a country feel to it.

Micah's immediate surroundings lay approximately halfway between Jerusalem and the region now known as the Gaza Strip, certainly a perennial news hot spot in our time. Back in Samuel and David's time, that region was where many skirmishes with the Philistines took place. Even though Micah seems to be an outsider, he does not completely avoid speaking of Judah's capital city and its temple. His prophetic oracles simply do not focus a significant emphasis on Jerusalem, as Isaiah does. He most likely was only an occasional visitor, not to mention the yearly pilgrimages up the hill to the temple in which he must have participated.

Similar Preaching

Whether those who heard the prophets lived in the big city or were abiding in the fields and folds of the countryside, both Isaiah and Micah proclaimed similar messages. (Compare, for instance, Micah 2:6–7 with Isaiah 6:9–10.) Both had words that promised destruction (Isaiah 3; 13; 24; 31; and 47; Micah 1–3; 5:10–15; and 6:9–16), and each predicted a future return of a small remnant of exile survivors (Isaiah 10:20–27; 14:1–2; 35; 45; and 49:8–26; Micah 4:6–13 and 5:7–9). There are remarkably similar sections in each prophet's book, even a near-verbatim parallel: Micah 4:1–3 is over 95 percent identical to Isaiah 2:2–4. The woes found in Micah 2 and Isaiah 5:8–23 are on the same wavelength, even though the specific examples of the peoples' faithlessness vary between the two prophets.

Where Micah complained about those who cry out "Peace!" only when it will be profitable to their stomachs (3:5), Isaiah called out the lunacy of those who split a block of wood—half to cook their food, and half to carve an idol before which they bow and pray (44:14–20). The man of Moresheth proclaimed that the Lord is far more pleased when the people follow His just decrees and act in mercy toward others, rather than offer the utmost in ceremonial worship and the show of symbolic gifts (Micah 6:6–8). And the prophet who had the ear of the king and frequented the temple was just as adamant about preserving justice for the needy, and he denounced those people who "honor [God] with their lips, while their hearts are far from [Him]" (Isaiah 29:13).

© iStockphoto.com

Pointing Forward to Jesus

Most important, these two prophets, who lived and worked in Judah at about the same time, joined in with the rest of "the goodly fellowship of the prophets" as they praised and confessed the promised Christ. Clearly, Isaiah took the lead, for he had the honor of extolling the Lord Immanuel (7:14), who was to be born of the Virgin and would also be a Prince of Peace (9:6) who would make a healing atonement for sinners as a Suffering Servant (53:5). Micah's contribution to the array of messianic prophecies was to predict Jesus' birth in Bethlehem (5:2a), a village that the prophet would probably have passed on the way up to Jerusalem. He also confessed that the Christ would not only have an ancient genealogy going back to David and Abraham but that He also would be the Son of God, begotten from eternity (5:2c).

Whether the prophets Isaiah and Micah were the stereotypical loners or close collaborators, they provide us a window into the world of their hearers. They exhibit many similarities and some key differences in emphasis as they proclaim Law and Gospel in Old Testament style. Their tandem witness to Christ makes clear to us even today that our acts of worship ought first to receive Him in faith and then diligently work out mercy for our neighbor. Many pages may separate them as far as our English Bible's contents are arranged, but Isaiah and Micah, along with their unique features, remain united in purpose, since the same Holy Spirit inspired them to write and thereby lead us to Jesus.

The Lord, My Shepherd

The profession of shepherd traces all the way back to Abel, the second person whose birth is recorded in the Bible. He was a keeper of sheep, a role itself derived from the original charge given to his father, Adam: "have dominion over . . . every living thing that moves on the earth" (Genesis 1:28). Shepherds are well-known in other ancient records besides the Bible, and symbolically, political leaders were often likened to shepherds keeping their sheep. For example, Hammurabi, the powerful Mesopotamian ruler and lawgiver, referred to himself as a shepherd for his subjects. Even though literal sheepherders were offensive to the Egyptians (Genesis 46:34), the coffin of King Tutankhamen was decorated with stylized shepherd's crooks. Many worthy people are given the honor of the title, but the ultimate shepherd is our Lord Himself (Psalm 23), who will feed, protect, and rescue His own people—the sheep of His pasture (Micah 7:14; Ezekiel 34).

Many people have never seen a shepherd in action. Can the biblical symbol of a shepherd still mean something to us today? If the concept of "follow the leader" is still easy enough to grasp in preschool, then it won't take too much extra effort to comprehend the thought of a flock of sheep gathering at the sound of their shepherd's voice (John 10:4). Even in our modern age, with all of its conveniences, complexities, and distractions, we still need—perhaps more than ever—a shepherd to call us by name, to feed, protect, and rescue us, so that we will not wander into spiritual danger, as sheep are prone to do.

He Feeds

The most urgent and constant need that a flock of sheep can have is for adequate pastureland. A shepherd can find himself in an extremely delicate situation if he must move on to find a better place to feed his sheep. If he drives them too hard, the weak and sick ones in the flock may fall back into danger or even die from exhaustion and malnourishment (see Genesis 33:13). Clearly, the better option, if available, is as Psalm 23:2 beautifully describes: to stay put in a green pasture of abundant, fresh grass, so that the flocks may lie down, consume as much as they need, and chew their cud with still water close by to drink.

Micah's prophetic dream is for the Lord to provide His people the ultimate shepherd's provisions: a forested, garden land (Micah 7:14). The mention of Bashan and Gilead refers to a region of the current kingdom of Jordan that is north of Amman, the capital. The "days of old" most likely was the time of Moses and Joshua, when two and a half tribes desired to inherit this land, even though it was located on the eastern side of the Jordan River, and not in the Promised Land that the rest of their relatives would possess. For as Numbers 32 attests, the land was so good for grazing that the fighting men of Reuben, Gad, and half of Manasseh promised to cross the Jordan and fight alongside the other tribes for land they would never inherit, in order to return to Gilead and Bashan to feed their flocks and livestock with its abundance. It's just a tiny glimpse of what the Lord, our Shepherd, has reserved for His own sheep once they complete their earthly battles and join the Church Triumphant!

He Protects

A shepherd cannot be timid in the face of danger. It seems as though the flock can approach the brink of death in less than a moment's notice. Enemies and predators are constant threats. Jesus pointed out that the shepherd's caring relationship with his sheep casts the deciding vote between running to personal safety like a hired hand and laying down his life to keep the flock from scattering (John 10:11–13). David was confident that the Lord would defeat Goliath through His unparalleled might, but David himself, based on his experience as a shepherd, was never afraid. He saw no real difference between the bombastic giant and an everyday lion or bear who would from time to time attempt an attack against him and his sheep (1 Samuel 17:34–37).

© iStockphoto.com

Our Good Shepherd protects His flock against the constant assaults of the devil, the sinful world, and even our own weak and self-centered human nature. He was prophesied to "shepherd His flock in the strength of the Lord. . . . And they shall dwell secure" (Micah 5:4). As for our enemies, even though they prey upon God's people like a lion in the midst of a flock, they shall be shepherded away from us with the sword (Micah 5:6, 8). We have the promise of everlasting protection when the Chief Shepherd sounds His voice and gathers His faltering flock around His pastor-preached Word, arming us with prayer that not only calls to Him in every trouble but also praises and gives thanks.

He Rescues

A dispersed flock aptly described the exiled people of Israel. They had disobeyed the Lord, and so He allowed surrounding enemy armies to scatter His sheep. The Assyrian wolf carried off the "lambs" of the Northern Kingdom of Israel; the Babylonians stole the Judean Southern Kingdom to increase their own folds. But the Lord reserved future rescue for them: "I will surely assemble all of you, O Jacob; I will gather the remnant of Israel; I will set them together like sheep in a fold, like a flock in its pasture, a noisy multitude of men" (Micah 2:12). God's house would become a "tower" for the flock, to which they would gather and receive salvation from the "hill of the daughter of Zion" (Micah 4:8). Jesus named His entire Christian Church, the elect drawn to Him from all nations of the world: "I have other sheep that are not of this fold. I must bring them also, and they will listen to My voice. So there will be one flock, one shepherd" (John 10:16).

The literal descendants of Israel were gathered back as a flock to the Promised Land, but eventually scattered again. Yet all who believe and turn to the Lord Jesus—Jew or Gentile—shall be rescued for the one true flock of Christendom. As one who has been baptized and called by the name that is above every name, you have been as a lost lamb that was saved from eternal danger. For He who once was silent as a sheep before the shearers now speaks His Word of forgiveness and peace that assures you: The Lord is your shepherd. You shall not want.

Little Town of Bethlehem

It's a familiar backdrop for the Sunday School Christmas pageant. A hilly village of simple dwellings beneath the wondrous Christmas star. Today, sadly, violence and poverty ravage this town that was once known for its deep and peaceful sleep. In the present century, an Israeli wall and fence system has dominated the site, designed to impede terrorism. This has led to other serious problems. Christians who cherish living near the place of Jesus' birth nevertheless must also constantly suffer the aftermath of the absolute worst expressions of human nature. Bethlehem has always been the unlikely place for God to do magnificent things, since from the days of antiquity until today; this place seems to embody the very antithesis of magnificence.

A Lowly Locale

In Hebrew, *beth-lehem* means "house of bread." Only a few miles south of Jerusalem, this shepherds' town borders the northern fringes of the Judean desert. Shepherding becomes a lot more difficult the farther south you go, due to the lack of vegetation. The Christmas story found this village overrun with visitors, descendants from its former glory days, forced to return by Caesar's tax decree. No room was available in the inn, so the little Lord Jesus had nowhere to lie but in a manger, a food box for animals.

So what do we have here? At the humblest location in the humblest town, which was named for ordinary bread, a lowly couple, which were nothing like the great kings of their ancestry, bring forth a lowly baby, who nevertheless is the majestic Son of God, Savior of the world! This was no accident, for this Almighty God and King is pleased to dwell in lowliness, to claim it as His own. Following His birth in Bethlehem, Jesus is further destined for a shameful cross.

Town of Tragedy

Bethlehem's biblical history goes far back, all the way to the Book of Genesis. Jacob, the third in line after his father, Isaac, and his grandfather Abraham, wrestled with God and received the name of Israel as a blessing. He and the many people and animals in his entourage then headed south

from Bethel on a hard journey, perhaps even using the same route that Mary and Joseph would travel many centuries later. When they reached the region of Ephrathah—which meant they were at or near the town of Bethlehem—Rachel, the woman whom Jacob loved and had worked for fourteen years to marry, was great with child, just as Mary would be at this location. On this journey southward, there had already been a death in their group, that of Rachel's nurse, Deborah; and 180-year-old Isaac, who had been blind for most of his life, was very close to breathing his last. But now, here at Ephrathah, tragedy struck as Rachel's labor hit her hard and she died delivering Benjamin. Jacob set up a pillar over her tomb along the road leading to Bethlehem. This was a monument of Jacob's love and sorrow, a landmark that was still there at the time of David and perhaps was there as Mary and Joseph passed by on that same road.

After the time of Moses and Joshua, and during the rule of Israel's Judges, Bethlehem surfaced again in Old Testament history. This time, the "house of bread" had an empty breadbasket. There was famine in the land, and Naomi and her husband and sons left for a foreign country in search of food. In the land of Moab, tragedy struck threefold as Naomi's husband and two sons died, leaving Naomi no option but to move back to Bethlehem in sorrow and brokenness. Only her also-widowed daughter-in-law Ruth traveled with her for comfort. But how could this foreign girl last through such heartache and struggle in Bethlehem? She had nothing more to gain from her mother-in-law, even in the impossible fantasy that Naomi could marry again and have another son who could grow up and marry Ruth.

Yet, on the road to Bethlehem, Ruth made a resolve to Naomi in what is now a well-known pledge: "Where you go I will go, where you lodge I will lodge. Your people shall be my people, and your God my God" (Ruth 1:16). Thus it was in Bethlehem that the wonderful story of redeeming love played out, where lowly, unlikely Ruth married the perfect match, Boaz. She became the great-grandmother of King David, and was an ancestor worthy of mention in the genealogy of Jesus Himself in the Gospel of Matthew (1:5).

Big Plans for Bethlehem

It was, of course, the little town of Bethlehem to which God sent Samuel the prophet to anoint King Saul's replacement. Samuel made the journey southward, tracing the same route of Jacob (also the future route of our Savior in Mary's womb), and his expectations were disappointed. Though he was the one called to speak for God, even he was misled by appearances. Among the strapping, noble, first seven sons of Jesse, not one would be God's choice for king. But the eighth son would be the Lord's Anointed One—little red-headed David who tended the sheep outside of Bethlehem, quite likely near the place where other shepherds much later would hear the song of the angels announcing Jesus' birth. So the unlikely, lowly candidate for Israel's great honor was selected king in lowly, unlikely Bethlehem, which you know from the Christmas story as the City of David.

About two hundred years after David's glorious reign, Micah pronounced his unique prophecy. In effect, he said, "Bethlehem, you are so small and insignificant that sometimes you don't even get counted. You are a reminder of failed expectations, empty stomachs, and grieving loved ones." But tiny, inadequate Bethlehem, with all of its history (some of it good, most of it sad), Bethlehem, the "house of bread," would shoot forth from its stump an eternal Savior, the Son of God, born of a virgin. To the King born in Bethlehem, the brothers and sisters of the Holy Christian Church will return as the new Israel, as sheep to be tended by the Good Shepherd, who spent at least His first night lying in a feed box. His mighty name will grant sustenance and peace to all Christians all over the world, even though the price of that peace meant pain and suffering for Him in His punishment for our sins. That's what awaits you, O little, sleepy town of Bethlehem!

Bethlehem for You

Can you identify with Bethlehem? Perhaps tragedy has struck your life, and your remembrance of it is like a permanent monument of sadness that you've erected in your heart. Maybe you were fooled by appearances, like Samuel. Or, like Naomi, your life feels bitter with emotional pain. Like the modern city of Bethlehem, you cannot avoid the nasty dividing wall of hostility between you and others, and it has just made things worse. As we examine ourselves and our lives according to God's Word, we find out that, just like Bethlehem, our Savior, Jesus Christ, came to us even though we had nothing in us worthy of a mighty Lord and King.

The eternal Son of God retraced our tragic journeys through life, just as He traveled the Bethlehem road, going right by Rachel's tomb while in the womb of Mary. Just as Ruth promised her undying dedication to weeping Naomi, your Savior, Immanuel, promises never to leave you nor forsake you. He forgives your sins and shortcomings; He heals your disappointments and hurts. Yes, Bethlehem is an insignificant village, beset with sin and weakness. But from such a lowly place came the Ruler, who rescued you with forgiveness, resurrection, and eternal life. The church where you hear His true Word and receive His Supper has now become for you the real house of bread!

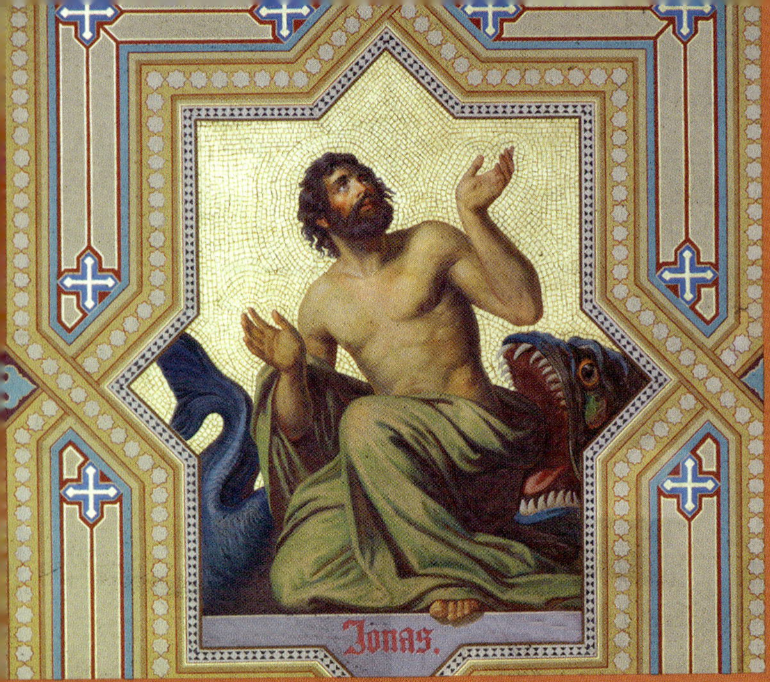

ANATOMY OF A COMPLAINT

Motivational speaker Will Bowen has been in high demand ever since 2007, when he envisioned a world that would become—with the help of his $1 purple bracelets and his mind-over-matter steps that they represent—free of all complaints. We instinctively know that complaining indicates that something is out of our control, and we become stressed out. Complaining is a sign of vulnerability. Complaints do not flow from a positive outlook on life, so we instinctively avoid them.

On the other end of the spectrum, some people have learned the art of wielding complaints as an effective weapon to achieve what they want. They are keenly tuned to the weaknesses of their targets. They "push the right buttons" and capitalize on what they hope will be a desire of the target to give in to the tantrum. The more this tactic is used, however, the more it runs the risk of placing great strain on relationships, which can be disastrous.

So complaints are both an obstacle to our emotional well-being and a sign of immaturity that achieves a few short-term goodies with many long-term consequences. Neither way looks good.

Biblical Complaining?

So why does the Bible encourage us to complain? It may not make any sense to us. For example, Jonah complained, knowing that the Lord would be merciful to Nineveh, claiming that was why he ran away in the first place. Job complained, even after his friends attempted to get him to stop, but then God restored everything above and beyond what he had initially lost. These two complaints sound similar, yet their results are very different from each other. How can we discern when it is appropriate to express our complaint and when it is not? What are our heavenly Father's directions for us when we have a complaint on our heart?

Faith: The Key Ingredient

Psalms is probably our best instruction book on how to complain to God. When you read some of these ancient songs, you might wonder at times whether the human authors were reverent enough. Consider these examples: "Has God forgotten to be gracious?" (Psalm 77:9); or "Why, O LORD, do You stand far away? Why do You hide Yourself in times of trouble?" (Psalm 10:1). Those cries sound distraught, uttered in the midst of despair as if the Lord meant only harm for the believer instead of good. Yet as you read these poetic laments, you find a decisive turn in their stories.

In the case of Psalm 77, you can perceive that the psalmist lifts up his head in hope in verses 10 and 11: "Then I said, 'I will appeal to this, to the years of the right hand of the Most High.' I will remember the deeds of the LORD; yes, I will remember Your wonders of old." What God had done in the past for His people Israel, He has also promised to do for His children today. He alone works wonders and also never changes; therefore, His faithful may direct their appeal straight to their heavenly Father through Him who sits at the right hand of the Most High, Jesus Christ, our Savior. The decisive turn in the complaint, then, is a confident faith in the Lord who has promised to hear, and believers yield to the only One who can vindicate us when the time is right. This is the kind of complaining that is pleasing to the Lord, because even though a believer complains, his faith nevertheless depends solely on God, and he trusts that God will come through according to His promise. When genuine faith is absent, however, the Lord hides His face from those who have turned to evil (Micah 3:4).

This is what leads to "bad" complaining, as in the case of Jonah. Similarly, the Israelites displeased the Lord when they grumbled against Moses in the wilderness (e.g., see Exodus 16:1–30 and Numbers 11:1–6, 18–23). Even though they were oppressed as slaves in Egypt, now that they were on their own, wandering through the wilderness. They longed for the fancy food that they enjoyed in the land of their overlords. When they complained about the "worthless" manna that they had to eat, it was clear that they coveted the gift and ignored the Giver. Without faith in the all-providing Lord, the complaint dissolves into a self-centered gripe. As you study Jonah's complaint over the Lord's mercy to the people of Nineveh (Jonah 4:1–4), notice the reluctant prophet's indictment against God. He was complaining precisely because the Lord is forgiving!

Sufficient Grace

What happens, though, when a believer's complaint includes genuine faith, the believer entrusts his entire life and situation into the heavenly Father's hands, and yet the believer sees no improvement? Micah questions, "Now why do you cry aloud? Is there no king in you?" (4:9) because now, in the midst of the Babylonian exile, the depths of sin's reality made God's rebellious people hit rock bottom. Difficult experiences in our Christian life remind us of St. Paul's repeated pleas to the Lord to remove the thorn that was thrust into his side (2 Corinthians 12:7–10). God's response, "My grace is sufficient for you, for My power is made perfect in weakness," is a hard lesson for us to learn at times. It doesn't seem right that a time of anguish could ever be a sign of God's love. In fact, the world never stops telling us the opposite—constant happiness is our ultimate goal. We even hear the opinion that God exists solely to keep us supplied with happiness, and if we are not happy, then we think we are getting punished.

Jesus' own disciples were dismayed when a horrific act of violence stunned the people of Galilee (Luke 13:1–9). When Jesus heard that Pontius Pilate had murdered a group of Galileans and mingled their blood with their sacrifices in Jerusalem, He queried His hearers: "Do you think that these Galileans were worse sinners than all the other Galileans, because they suffered in this way? No, I tell you; but unless you repent, you will all likewise perish" (vv. 2–3). He recalled another disaster—the fall of a tower in Siloam that killed eighteen people—and made the same conclusion for them too. Our moments of suffering are not signs of rejection from God, that He will never answer us again; rather, they are gracious inducements to turn to Him for help, forgiveness, and strength. Micah presented his inspired predictions of destruction, and then he complained, mourned, and lamented what was about to befall his fellow citizens of Judah (Micah 1:8–9; 2:7–8; 7:1–7). His complaints were then answered by the promises of God's love and rescue (Micah 4; 5:7–15; 7:18–20).

The Greatest Complaint

When Jesus Himself complained on the cross, "My God, My God, why have You forsaken Me?" (Mark 15:34), He collected all our complaints, including those of prophets like Obadiah, Jonah, and Micah, and set them front-and-center before the heavenly Father. Our Savior is the only one who was truly rejected—not just by other men, but also by God Himself—and it happened for our benefit. Even while suffering in the most horrible way on the cross, He trusted in His Father's deliverance from death; and He was raised on the third day so that His flesh never saw the corruption that awaits all our bodies (see Acts 2:22–32). Because of Him, we too shall rise to incorruption, and our complaints will receive their final and most gracious answer.

Prophets like Obadiah, Jonah, and Micah could only hope and trust that the Lord would fulfill their prophecies. We who are in Christ see their fulfillment. Although we may complain still, lifting weary voices in prayer, Christ assures us of deliverance. Pray to your Lord today with all sincerity. For He intercedes for you.

God's on the MOUNTAIN

What else in all of God's visible creation can bear a greater testimony to His utter majesty than mountains? Their grand scale can be quite mesmerizing. Even when looking down on them from an airplane window at 30,000 feet, you can still be filled with awe at these magnificent ripples that our Creator folded into the earth's crust. Many a "bucket list" includes hiking or climbing up to a mountain's summit. Their towering height seems to exude control over all that lies before them, including the climate: on one side of a mountain, you may find a forested paradise; on the other, an arid desert.

When clouds hide a mountaintop from view, it is easy to understand why mountains were considered points of intersection between heaven and earth since the beginning of recorded history. When you stand on the peak, the air feels cleaner and cooler. You almost get a floating sensation, and you hear a perfect silence that shuts out the frantic world crawling in circles below you. References to mountains as epicenters of God's mighty works of majesty are prolific in both the Old and New Testaments. Pull on your hiking boots and let's explore some of the ways in which they reveal to us the God of our salvation!

© iStockphoto.com

Don't Touch the Mountain!

At first it may seem like a contradiction that an omnipresent God would be limited to high elevations. Wasn't that the fallacy that led to the downfall of Babel in Genesis 11? The people of Babel figured that if they could establish themselves with a city and tower that reached to the heavens—that is, up to God's realm—then that would "make a name" for themselves and they would not be scattered. Yet the problem that the Lord had with the people of Babel was not that they thought of Him as dwelling on high but rather that they desired to achieve greatness to the exclusion of faith in His promises. Indeed, they perceived majesty in the mountains that God created; they wanted to take pride in a "mountain" made by their own hands.

Surely, the Lord was with His faithful believers wherever they were, not just when they climbed up a mountain. For when the children of Israel languished in Egyptian slavery and cried out to Him, He heard them. His master plan of salvation was set in motion when He contacted runaway Moses by means of the burning bush on Mount Horeb, also known as Sinai. Even though God was everywhere, He wanted to establish a point of contact between His grace and the intended objects of His grace: sinful mankind. He gave a sign for Moses: "When you have brought the people out of Egypt, you shall serve God on this mountain" (Exodus 3:12). It was a limitation that the Lord was willing to set upon Himself in order to demonstrate His loving purpose for an undeserving, yet chosen people.

Just as a mountain was an access point to grace, it was also an imposing barrier from God's absolute holiness. Evil cannot exist in His presence, no matter how much He loves the person doing evil. The sinner, as a sinner, must be kept away until atonement is made; and only by faith in Christ will the sinner be cleansed and then admitted. This was just as much true for Old Testament believers, who were commanded, "Take care not to go up into the mountain or touch the edge of it. Whoever touches the mountain shall be put to death" (Exodus 19:12). Mount Sinai then became known as a symbol for Law and God's judgment. The people trembled at the foot of the mountain when the Lord made it quake with His massive glory. His ultimate goal was not to condemn—He still desired to save His children and bring them close, but distance was necessary first.

When Jonah announced his message of divine punishment against Nineveh, he watched with great anticipation from a close-by mountain. He may have allowed his imagination to run wild as he looked down on the repenting city from the east, with the first glimpse of sunrise to his back, awaiting the city's forty-day deadline.

This elevated vantage point would assure Jonah a front-row seat when divine retribution would perhaps strike in the early morning hours, similar to the fire and brimstone that destroyed Sodom and Gomorrah in Genesis 19. On that Assyrian summit, far from any of the mountains of Israel, the Lord revealed to Jonah His mercy instead of condemnation, much to the prophet's dismay.

Lift Up Your Eyes to the Hills

Another mountain that stands in contrast to Sinai is what came to be called Mount Zion, the centerpiece of Jerusalem and eventual site of the temple. Instead of rumbling thunder and the mandatory distance from utter holiness, this mountain would be set aside to offer forgiveness out of the abundance of God's mercy. Its history began with Genesis 22, in which the Lord tested Abraham and commanded him to sacrifice his promised son, Isaac, on what was at the time named Mount Moriah. Centuries later, after David captured the fortress of Zion from the Jebusites and established his capital city, he purchased a nearby plot of ground that included this mountain and built an altar on the place where the Lord relented from a deadly plague that was ravaging His kingdom (2 Samuel 24:10–25). Since it was not given to David to build the stationary house of the Lord (2 Samuel 7), he reserved the site of that altar for Solomon's massive temple project.

Once the Lord's house was completed, Solomon dedicated this most important of high places, offering the prayer that is recorded in 1 Kings 8. Included in his prayer is the ponderous question, "But will God indeed dwell on the earth? Behold, heaven and the highest heaven cannot contain You; how much less this house that I have built!" (1 Kings 8:27). For that matter, no mountain could do the job either. However, the point of the question reminds us that "God's house" refers to not a place of residence but a location where God chooses to be found for the good of those who seek Him. For generations to follow, pilgrims traveled up the mountain slope toward Jerusalem and the temple. As they ascended, the faithful sang psalms that extolled the One who at that particular place promised deliverance: "I lift up my eyes to the hills. From where does my help come? My help comes from the LORD, who made heaven and earth" (Psalm 121:1–2).

Not far from the temple mount, and a long time after Solomon's original temple was destroyed, another mountain became the place where the Lord achieved true, permanent deliverance. This was Golgotha, the Place of a Skull, which through its Latin translation gives us the well-known title Mount Calvary. This is the mountain on which Jesus Christ, the Son of Man, was raised up, that all who believe in Him will have eternal life (see John 3:14–16). The events of Golgotha supersede and fulfill everything else that God has done for the world on any other mountain. Christ's completed mission of death and resurrection atoned for all sin, reconciling the world with God. It also laid the foundation for the true Church, the new Mount Zion, which is now spread throughout the world and no longer in one particular place (see John 4:21–24). Obadiah praised what for him would be a future development. He proclaimed: "Saviors shall go up to Mount Zion to rule Mount Esau, and the kingdom shall be the LORD's" (v. 21). Those who praise Jesus Christ and confess His name are bestowed with the title "saviors," and Mount Esau, the prophet's chosen term for all who rebel against God, shall fall to the ultimate triumph of the Church.

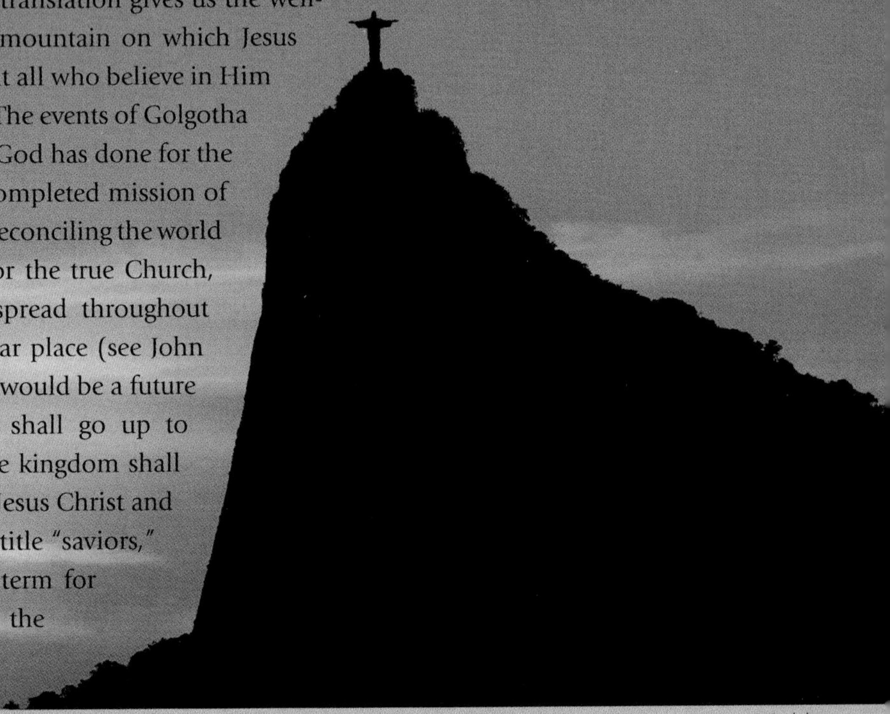

Perfection with High Elevation

You would think that the Garden of Eden might have been situated higher than its surroundings, if not on a mountain itself, given that four rivers issued forth from its single stream (see Genesis 2:10–14). And thanks to the accomplishment achieved on Mount Calvary, Scripture comforts us with the assurance of a return to an even better Eden in the new creation that will begin at the end of time. The final chapters of Revelation depict a "great, high mountain" (Revelation 21:10), upon which New Jerusalem descends and from which the river of life flows.

Old Testament prophets caught a glimpse of this ultimate, end-time mountain too. Micah 4 rejoices in the "mountain of the house of the LORD" (v. 1) and that in its shadow "nation shall not lift up sword against nation, neither shall they learn war anymore" (v. 3). The contrast is especially striking, given that already in Micah 3 the prophet had predicted the destruction of the temple on the literal mountain in Jerusalem. Isaiah was privileged to see the future glory of the exalted mountain on which God will "swallow up death forever" (Isaiah 25:8). Zechariah (8:1–8) extols Jerusalem's "holy mountain" and paints a picture of what everyday life would look like in its streets. Ezekiel's symbolic temple and surrounding ideal city that he saw and described in chapters 40–48 center our gaze of faith upon a very high mountain. You think mountains are huge and majestic now? Then you're really going to like what you will see when all that God has promised comes to its final fulfillment!